T0164806

Other books by the same author

Secrets of Successful Marriages
How to Discover God's Will for Your Life
Wisdom: Your Key to Success
Choosing the Best: Living for What Really Matters
Matthew 1-15: A Pentecostal Commentary
Matthew 16-28: A Pentecostal Commentary
Mark: A Pentecostal Commentary
Luke 1-11: A Pentecostal Commentary
Luke 12-24: A Pentecostal Commentary
John 1-11: A Pentecostal Commentary
John 12-21: A Pentecostal Commentary
Romans: A Pentecostal Commentary
1 Corinthians: A Pentecostal Commentary
2 Corinthians: A Pentecostal Commentary
Ephesians: A Pentecostal Commentary
Galatians: A Pentecostal Commentary
Philippians and Titus: A Pentecostal Commentary
Colossians and Philemon: A Pentecostal Commentary
1 & 2 Thessalonians: A Pentecostal Commentary
1 & 2 Timothy: A Pentecostal Commentary
Hebrews: A Pentecostal Commentary
James and Jude: A Pentecostal Commentary
1 & 2 Peter: A Pentecostal Commentary
1-3 John: A Pentecostal Commentary
Revelation: A Pentecostal Commentary

ENEMIES of Your Marriage

DR. MATTHEW N.O. SADIKU

Order this book online at www.trafford.com
or email orders@trafford.com

Most Trafford titles are also available at major online book retailers.

Print information available on the last page.

ISBN: 978-1-4907-8965-1 (sc)
ISBN: 978-1-4907-9115-9 (hc)
ISBN: 978-1-4907-8968-2 (e)

Trafford rev. 10/23/2018

www.trafford.com

North America & international
toll-free: 1 888 232 4444 (USA & Canada)
fax: 812 355 4082

To my wife Kikelomo

who has been a wonderful gift!

Contents

Preface

The divorce rate in America affects about half of all marriages. Divorce rates among born-again Christians are 27% higher than for non-born-again Christians. This clearly shows that building a successful, long-lasting marriage is not easy.

It does not matter where you are, what you have been through, or the current situation of your marriage, there is hope. God designed marriage to include you, your spouse, and Him. Without God, the Designer of marriage, you are lost in your quest for marital happiness. According to God's plan, marriage is to be enjoyed, not endured. Your marriage will thrive and succeed if you do things God's way. Don't try to reinvent the wheel. Learn from other people's experience by reading this book in your hand.

In my former book on marriage, *Secrets of Successful Marriages,* I shared ten principles that will make your marriage work and be successful. In this book, *Enemies of Your Marriage,* I am sharing what will not make your marriage thrive. I have identified twelve enemies of your marriage. There are forces working against the success of the marriage. These enemies will truncate the life of your marriage if care is not taken. They may cause you not to enjoy the marriage and eventually lead to divorce. A marriage is successful if the couple live together happily until death separates them. The book helps you identify problem areas of your marriage and how you can overcome them. If you address these problems or avoid them altogether, you will enjoy your marriage and be happy.

I would like to express my profound appreciation for my wife Kikelomo, Dr. Solomon Lekia, and Dr. Kareem Olarenwaju for reviewing the maniscript.

Introduction

To stay happily married is getting harder and harder these days. All marriages face problems. Couples must work together in solving the problems and saving their marriage.

The author has identified twelve common problems in marriage that husbands and wives should guard against.

- Selfishness
- Lack of love and affection
- Worldliness
- Materialism
- The devil
- Irresponsibility
- Mixed faith
- Nagging and criticism
- Infidelity
- Unforgiveness
- Bitterness and Resentment
- Overcommitment

Selfishness is basically insisting in your way or insisting on your rights. Love does not insist on its own way (1 Corinthians 13:4). Lack of love and affection is the cousin of selfishness. We cannot produce optimally where we are not loved and celebrated. Worldliness is choosing worldly priorities and spending most of our time and energy pursuing wrong goals. Materialism is a mindset that desires to make money and spend it on material things, to the neglect of spiritual matters. Satan is our chief enemy. We should be sensitive to his operation in our marriage. We should not be ignorant of his devices (2 Corinthians 2:11). Irresponsibility is not accepting responsibility for our actions.

It is difficult to cope with issues, pray, raise kids, etc. when the couple are of different faith. Criticize sparingly and avoid nagging as much as possible. Infidelity is breaking a promise to remain faithful to a sexual partner. Each person should enter marriage realizing that your spouse is not perfect and is going to offend you. You must be willing to forgive just as God forgives us (Ephesians 5:32). Bitterness and resentment develop as a result of offenses committed by your spouse and not forgiving them. Being overcommitted to other things and not spending enough time with your spouse defeats the purpose of marriage (avoiding loneliness).

These common problems can be avoided, fixed or resolved using many tips offered in this book. They are regarded as enemies of your marriage. These problems do not happen overnight; they creep up on your marriage gradually. If you identify them in your marriage, you should be able to do something about them before it is late. Seek professional help if necessary.

Unfortunately most couples divorce without knowing that their marriage problems can be solved. If you address them or avoid them, you will enjoy your marriage and be happy. Your marriage will never experience divorce.

CHAPTER 1

Selfishness

> *"Don't be selfish; don't live to make a good impression on others. Be humble, thinking of others as better than yourself"* (Philippians 2:3,4, TLB).

Before you marry, you only have one person to think about—yourself. But marriage has changed all that. Now, you should put the needs of your spouse above your wants. For a marriage to be happy, we must avoid certain things which are enemies of happy, successful marriages. The number one enemy of your marriage is selfishness. As Oscar Wilde said, "Selfishness is not living as one wishes to live, it is asking others to live as one wishes to live."

In our society, selfishness reigns. This should not surprise us because the Bible says that in the last days men and women will be "lovers of themselves" (2 Timothy 3:2). There are forces in our culture today that contribute and encourage selfish behaviors. These include pornography, two-career families, and the dynamics of the blended family. Marriage is not designed for selfish individuals. And God does not answer the prayer of selfish people. For example, if you pray that your spouse will die so that you claim life insurance, God will not hear you.

MANIFESTATIONS OF SELFISHNESS

Selfishness is doing things your own way or insisting on your rights. A selfish person is mainly concerned for his or her own personal welfare without taking into consideration the welfare of others. Sometimes one can show qualities of selfishness without even realizing it. A person's behavior may be selfishly motivated without knowing it. These are the common signs of a selfish spouse:

- He cares only about his needs in bed.
- He is only interested in what pleases him; he does not help with the house chores.
- He interrupts when you speak.
- He pays no attention to details.
- He cares more about career than character.
- Even when he realizes he is wrong, he does not know how to apologize and ask for forgiveness.
- She always blames others for her problems and thinks she is ok.
- She hides something she is ashamed of.
- She is sentimental, not objective.
- She keeps blaming others for her failures.

Selfishness demonstrates itself in many other ways: not praying together, having separate bank accounts, pursuing separate goals, not agreeing on the number of children to have, one eats meat while another eats chicken, one lives in Africa while the other lives in America, living as if the other doesn't exist.

Selfishness shows up in claiming entitlement or pursuing my rights. This is the feeling that I deserve something or it is my right to have a good marriage because I deserve it.

Selfishness also manifests itself as stubbornness, the sin of witchcraft. It also manifests itself in rationalization.

- What makes a teenager kill her mom? Selfishness.
- What makes a husband kill his wife? Selfishness.
- What prevents a person from taking care of their parents at old age? Selfishness.
- What makes a couple not to be willing to raise children? Selfishness.

THE EFFECTS OF SELFISHNESS

Selfishness in any relationship can be toxic. Some of the effects of selfishness in marriage include:

- It is perhaps the most dangerous threat to oneness in marriage.
- It repels others from you and creates an atmosphere of hatred.
- It makes it difficult to compromise.
- It leads to marital problems such as sexual issues, communication, and in-law issues.
- It affects your happiness in marriage as it interferes with healthy selflessness which is the essence of marital love.
- It prevents a couple from having the same goals.
- It can cause an inability to maintain a healthy loving relationship.
- It can prevent parents from being responsible for the kids.
- It can lead to conflict, strife, infidelity, separation and divorce.

Someone once said, "Selfsihness is a fantastic way to be miserable."

LOVE: THE ANTIDOTE TO SELFISHINESS

Selfishness is insisting on your rights, while love does not insist on its own way (1 Coritnthians.13:4). Selfishness is all about getting, while love is all about giving. We must consider others better and emulate Christ's example (Philippians 2:3-5). Selfishness causes disunity, disagreement, and separation in marriages.

Overcoming selfishness in a marriage takes time. It requires years of selfless love towards your partner. I suggest that you take the following actions.

1. Prioritize Your Spouse:

The first step in overcoming selfishness is learning to put yourself second and prioritize your partner's needs before your own. Like Paul said, "Let each of you look not only to his own interests, but also to the interests of others" (Philippians 2:4). We must learn to prioritize our spouse over ourselves. As husbands, we are called to a higher standard that demands laying down our lives for our wives (Ephesians 5:25). Think about her needs above yours. Making her happy increases your own happiness. Make regular deposits into the memory banks of your spouse and children. They will never forget it.

Serving our husbands with a humble heart speaks volumes. Proverbs 14:1 says, "The wise woman builds her house, but the foolish tears it down with her own hands." God's plan is that we treasure and cultivate our marriages. Since selfishness results in being independent, sharing and giving to a spouse can be effective in breaking the chains of independence.

2. Fight Against Pride

As Mark Merrill rightly said, "Selfishness destroys relationships, humility develops relationships." Fight against pride by remembering that everything you have including your spouse comes from God. Your desire to serve and your commitment to serve all come from God. Find small ways to serve your spouse—doing the dishes, making the bed, etc. Abraham showed a humble, selfless love toward his nephew Lot by allowing Lot to choose first (Genesis 13:5-13). As Abraham exemplified, we should not seek their own good, but the good of others (1 Corinthians 10:24). As you let Jesus have His rightful place in your life, there will be less selfishness, less drama, less pride, and less me.

3. Learn to Compromise

Couples must understand that when they marry, it is a matter of give and take from both sides. Being selfless and loving may mean compromising. Cultivate the habit of compromising when you cannot agree on something. Let go of the need to be right or always get your way. Compromises bring you closer together.

CONCLUSION

Act more like a teammate in your marriage and less like an adversary. Commit to playing cooperatively versus competitively. Become a team player in your marriage. Unity is the goal of Christian marriage. God wants the husband and wife to be united in purpose to glorify Him while maintaining their uniqueness. That goal cannot be achieved with selfishness but with love; love is selfless, not selfish. If you pursue this goal, you will enjoy your marriage and be happy. As Albert Einstein rightly said, "Only a life lived for others is a life worthwhile."

CHAPTER 2

Lack of Love and Affection

"Don't just pretend that you love others: really love them. Hate what is wrong. Stand on the side of the good. Love each other with brotherly affection and take delight in honoring each other" (Romans 12:9,10).

Healthy relationships are important to individuals and to society as a whole. Lack of love and affection in marriage can be a grave misfortune to any man or woman because it deprives them of one the greatest joys life has to offer. This deprivation is an enemy of marriage and it may surely destroy the relationship.

Although no relationship is perfect, affection is an important part of any loving relationship. It is the verbal and physical expression of the love, warmth and caring you and your partner feel for each other. It allows us to connect to another person by showing our feelings.[1]

Couples who lack love and affection are not alone in their struggles. Many couples endure similar headache. A man or woman may feel unloved for a variety of reasons. The absence of affection gives them a sense of insecurity from which they naturally want to escape. A man or woman may make desperate efforts to win their spouse's affection. As Albert Einstein said, "Women marry men hoping that the man will change. Men marry women hoping that the woman will change. Inevitable, both end up disappointed."

AFFECTION DEFICIT

Here are some of the signs indicating a lack of affection or affection deficit in a marriage[2]:

1. There is no spark of playfulness between you
2. There are little or no displays of mutual gratitude
3. Communication mostly centers on the mundane
4. There is little or no touch between you
5. You talk negatively about your partner to others
6. You feel you don't love your partner any more

Women tend to love men for their character, while men love woman for their appearance. Just as our body craves for food, water, and rest, our entire being craves affection.

Affection can be one of the first things to go when a marriage is in trouble. If you are craving affection in your marriage and are longing to be hugged, kissed, or given affection through caring words such as "I love you," you are not alone.

ROOT CAUSES OF LACK OF AFFACTION

The root causes of the pain must be addressed before your relationship can move forward to a healthier, happier, more intimate place.

Any marriage can be saved from a lack of affection provided the couple wants to improve or change. At the foundation of overcoming lack of love and affection is the couple's desire to preserve the marriage and family.

The first step toward recovery is to confront harmful ways of thinking and behaving, and replace them with healthier methods. Learn to seek appropriate counselors or pastors, resources such as books, videos, and couples' workshops.

Begging for affection feels terrible, even if your man or woman comply! So my advice is: don't do it. Fretting about a lack of affection won't help you save a marriage or make your marriage more affectionate. It is better to focus on what you *can* control.

INCREASING YOUR LOVE AND AFFECTION

Here are some ways to enhance your love and affection. These are tips that make relationships survive and thrive.

1. Communication: You should be able to talk to your partner about anything—the good and the bad. This is important for a healthy relationship. In your communication, be honest, truthful, and open with your partner. It is important to be able to talk together without fearing how the other person will respond or if you will be judged. For example, if you want your partner to be more loving and affectionate with their words, feel free to let them know. Affectionate communication has many benefits such as intimacy, satisfaction, commitment, and long-term survival.

2. Commitment: Love is a voluntary, intelligent choice, made in the full knowledge that the opposite choice (selfishness) is always possible. It is a commitment of the will. Commitment is the glue of marriage. It is having the intention to persist in a relationship. It is what makes a relationship strong. It is what your marriage vows are all about. It may involve taking responsibility for your actions and words. It may also involve spending time together or just talking together.[3] The amount of affection you express to your partner best predicts your commitment. Sometimes, you need to verbally communicate your commitment to your partner. Remember, you are the one who gains when you are highly committed to your marriage.

3. Respect: You need to mutually respect each other. If respect is present in your relationship, your partner will value your beliefs, opinions, and who you are as a person. You should treat each other as equal partners. You have the same say in making decisions. This will make you and your partner feel important and respected.

4. *Physical affection*: To avoid your relationship becoming routine, make effort to be more romantic or affectionate. Physical affection is an important aspect of romantic relationships. Different ways you can show affection include hugging, massaging, caressing, cuddling, holding hands, kissing on the lips, kissing on the face, and touching. Other ways include a greeting card or an "I love you" note; a bouquet of flowers; phone calls; and conversations with thoughtful and loving expressions. Recent research has shown that increased kissing in relationships is linked to *decreases* in cholesterol. Physical touch is also a key factor to a lasting relationship. Showing physical affection enhances closeness and commitment. This increases relationship satisfaction which in turn leads to greater sexual satisfaction. There is less conflict in romantic relationships when partners treat each other with physical affection.

CONCLUSION

Hopefully with these tips, you can stir your marriage in the right direction and feel like your relationship is growing in a positive way. Great marriages do not happen by coincidence. They are the result of a consistent investment of time, affection, forgiveness, and commitment between a husband and a wife. Love is a decision, not a feeling or infatuation. Understand your spouse's basic needs and be willing to do your best to meet them. Show love in words and deeds. When your wife is truly loved as Christ expects you, when she knows that she means more to you than anything or anyone else, she will fully surrender. Someone has said, "A woman will leave you for lack of attention and affection quicker than she would if you cheated on her."

NOTES

1 M. T. Hill, "Intimacy, passion, commitment, physical affection and relationship stage as related to romantic relationship satisfaction," *Doctoral Dissertation*, Oklahoma State University, May 2009.

2 Rich Nicastro, "Strengthen Your Relationship," http://www.strengthenyourrelationship.com/free-relationship-resources/free-relatio\nship-advice-articles/relationship-advice-does-your-relationship-suffer-from-affection-deficit-disorder/

3 M. N. O. Sadiku, *Secrets of Successful Marriages*. Philadelphia, PA: Covenant Publishers, 1991, p. 232.

CHAPTER 3

Worldliness

> *"Do not love the world or anything in the world. If anyone loves the world, love for the Father is not in them. For everything in the world—the lust of the flesh, the lust of the eyes, and the pride of life—comes not from the Father but from the world"* (1John 2:15,16).

The Christian marriage stands in great danger from the forces of worldliness and materialism. Worldliness is a terrible problem for mankind and for marriage particularly. Worldliness is a dangerous enemy of yours and your marriage. Any Christian who lives in America is susceptible to this terrible plague of worldliness. Christians are not opposed to making money or making their way in this world. We are not indifferent to improving oneself through education or training. What we are opposed is choosing the wrong priorities in life and spending most of our time and energy pursuing the wrong goals. Let us begin this chapter by clarifying what worldliness is all about.

WHAT IS WORDLINESS?

There are two ways of viewing reality: through the prism of the world, and through the prism of the Spirit. We are either predominantly worldly or godly. The way of the world is hostile to the things of God and 180 degrees removed from the love of righteousness. Worldliness is the love of beauty without a corresponding love of righteousness. According to Jesus, the world's way seems to be appealing, broader, and easier (Matthew 7:13).

Worldliness is not a matter of do's and don'ts. Rather it is a matter of the attitude of the heart, a particular way of thinking and dealing with things. Worldliness manifests itself in our lives in the following ways.

1. Worldly mindset: Worldliness is a man-centered way of thinking. It is to be secular, unspiritual, materialistic, and irreligious. It is the mindset of the unregenerate. It is nothing more than self-centeredness. It urges us to get what we want, when we want it, and how we want it. It is focused on self, not on God or others. For example, if a lady wears a new dress in church in order to attract attention, that is worldliness. If a man must buy a new car every year in order to keep up with the style, that is worldliness.

Worldliness operates from the flesh, which lusts against the Spirit (Galatians 5:17) and the carnal mind which is hostile to God. It judges the importance of things by material results. It measures success by numbers.[1] This is fundamentally the basic difference between the person of faith and the unbeliever. The unbeliever judges things by worldly standards, by his senses, and by time. The believer brings God into everything, viewing things from His perspective.

To avoid cultivating the worldly mindset of their neighbors, God specifically told Israel not to act like other nations (Jeremiah 10:2). They paid no attention to this in many ways. They asked for a king to lead them like other nations (1 Samuel 8:5). They were involved in evil practices exceeding the pagan nations they displaced (2 Chronicles 33:10). God was so angry with them that He sent them into exile (1 Chronicles 9:1).

2. *Worldly Wisdom:* The wisdom that comes from the world is earthly, unspiritual, and demonic (James 3:15). It's sometimes tempting to follow the advice of worldly wisdom because many times it seems to make sense—at least from man's point of view. Worldly wisdom thrives in the culture of lies and deception. The world promises to make people happy with pleasures, materialism, and instant gratification. Yet the world's wisdom only leads down the road of disappointment, regret, and pain.

3. *Friendship with the World:* The whole world's system is anti-God. It generates and sustains our government, entertainment, fashion, business, healthcare, education, technology, and legal system. It profoundly affects our belief systems, values, and attitudes, and these in turn have shaped our conduct.[2] Worldliness is being more concerned about worldly affairs than spiritual things. It is the exact opposite of godliness. Paul equates worldliness with spiritual immaturity in 1 Corinthians 3:1-3. Demas deserted Paul because of worldliness (2 Timothy 4:10).

Friendship with the world is hatred toward God (James 4:4). We cannot love both God and the world. We must make a choice. Paul said, "Do not copy the behavior and customs of this world, but be a new and different person with a fresh newness in all you do and think" (Romans 12:2, TLB). We should be *in* the world and yet not *of* the world. We should not fear what the people of the world fear or become like them (Isaiah 8:12, NIV). The tragedy is that when we become like the world, we lose all our power to influence the world.

4. *Satan's influence*: Satan is the god of this world (2 Corinthians 4:4). Worldliness is Satan's use of idols such as pride, selfishness, and pleasure to maintain his dominion over men and women. It is one of the greatest challenges facing churches today. Worldliness thrives in the environment of lies and deception, which are the tools of Satan. Instead of the churches transforming the culture, the reverse has happened. Unconsciously, churches have been converted to the world through worldliness. The church is asleep spiritually and not paying attention. Satan has designed ways of life that are fast-paced, filled with an array of sense-appealing entertainments, fashions, and gadgets. Because of its subtle attractiveness and magnetism, worldliness has impressed itself upon God's people and had a stronghold on most marriages. Much of the spiritual deadness and complacency in our churches and marriages finds its roots in worldliness.

Other ways worldliness manifests itself include worldly manners (2 Corinthians 1:17), worldly passions (Titus 2:11,12), worldly cares (Matthew 6:25-33), and worldly love (1 John 2:15).[3]

CONSEQUENCES OF WORLDLINESS

Worldliness has some negative effects on your marriage and your soul. These include loving the world, accumulating materials unnecessarily, and hostility toward marriage.

1. *Loving the world:* Worldliness withdraws our affections from the nobler things and fixes them on earthly things. Christians are warned not to love the world (1 John 2:15). The world is a cosmos, a system apart from God, being organized and regulated according to ungodly principles and false values. Loving the world is having a lingering desire to be part of the world after one has been saved from it by Christ. It is becoming seduced again by the very things that once held us captive.

According to 1 John 2:15-17, worldliness is the lust of the flesh (sensualism), worldliness is the lust of the eyes (materialism), and worldliness is the pride of life (egotism).[4] Worldliness makes us engaged with the world in an ungodly manner. It focuses our attention on earthly "accomplishments" and material possessions -- cars, homes, clothes, gold, diamonds, money, beautiful women, etc. It distracts our attention from preparing for Christ's return and makes us focus on worldly things.

We should remember Lot's wife. She looked back, revealing that her heart was still to be in Sodom, a type of the world. She reluctantly left Sodom because she loved the world, not having the faith in what the angel told her (Genesis 19:26). She gradually believed that the angel's expectations were too exacting and difficult and she suddenly died.

2. *Materialism:* Worldliness gives birth to materialism. Materialism has compelled mankind to pursue unsatiable desires and unbounded greed to achieve more and more which results in a disgraceful life of immorality, immodesty, pornography, drugs, child abuse, women abuse, divorce, and other kinds of social misbehavior. Man has become obsessed with striving for more comfort, more material goods, greater power over his fellow men, and unceasing technological progress. Advertising (a tool of 'phenomenon of consumerism') has been accused of promoting and glamorizing values that are materialistic and self-centered. Advertisers have focused more on people who yearn to be free from all restraints and responsibilities.[5] Christmas is a good example of the world's power of attraction through advertising. It plays upon all of a person's senses with

pleasant music, lights, colors, foods, clothes, gifts, and parties. It is an attractive trap to worldliness.

This passionate, unrestrained pursuit of material goods, to the exclusion of everything else, bars man from all spiritual insight and close walk with God. It leads to a lack of satisfaction, frustration, unhappiness, a lack of fulfillment, and confusion.

3. *Enemy of marriage*: Worldliness has a power that produces an intriguing result in marriages. Marriage has become materialistic. Marriage is regarded as a means to an end and an end in itself in the everlasting struggle for status and stuff. Some people think sexual pleasure is the most important thing in the world. Sex is awesome and wonderful, but we should not make it a god.

OVERCOMING WORDLINESS

Identifying what worldliness is one thing, battling it is quite another. To escape worldliness, we must apply God's way of escape. We must develop a strong faith, focus on things above, share things with others, and be watchful.

1. *Develop a strong faith*: Faith is the victory over the world because through our faith we let go of the world and cleave totally to Jesus. "For whatever is born of God overcomes the world. And this is the victory that has overcome the world—our faith." (1 John 5:4). Faith comes as God's world is implanted into our hearts (James 1:21). "Do not love the world or the things in the world. If anyone loves the world the love of the Father is not in him" (1 John 2:15).

2. *Focus on the things above*: To escape worldliness Christians are taught to: (1) avoid a love of the world (1 John 2:15-17), (2) keep yourself pure and clean (1 Timothy 5:22), (3) put to death sinful habits (Colossians 3:5-6), (4) say "no" to ungodliness and worldly passions (Titus 2:11-12), and (5) seek the things that are above (Colossians 3:1).[6] God actually demands that we have more allegiance to Him than to the members of our own families (Matthew 10:37-39). We must not let the world around us squeeze us into its own mold (Romans 12:2).

If we truly love God, worldly things would not have much appeal. We should no longer seek the things that are of the earth – the lust of the flesh, lust of the eyes, and pride of life. We are now to align ourselves fully with our citizenship in heaven. We must live as though our home were in heaven (I Peter 2:11). Our longing to commune with Christ and maintain a good relationship with Him should control all that we do.

3. *Share with others*: God is not against His people prospering or even getting rich. For example, Abraham, David, and Solomon were all wealthy beyond imagination. We are only trustees or stewards of all God has given us and we are expected to be faithful in distributing the wealth (1 Corinthians 4:2). God wants us to share what we have with others including the poor, needy, widows, orphans, foreigners, etc. God is most concerned about how we use our wealth to further His kingdom and how we fare in our relationships with our spouses and others.

4. *Be watchful*: We must constantly realize that as long as we live on this planer earth we are in enemy territory (John 17:15, 1 Peter 5:8). To avoid being useless in our life and ineffective in our marriage, we need to be watchful and spend time in prayer. The enemy uses worldliness to undermine our faith and corrupt the truth. There are several things in this world that fight for our time and can make us lose our focus. Supernatural influence has to be met with supernatural power: 'For though we walk in the flesh, we do not war according to the flesh. For the weapons of our warfare are not carnal but mighty in God for pulling down strongholds' (2 Corinthians 10:3-4).

CONCLUSION

Worldliness is one of the most dangerous enemies of a believer and one of the greatest enemies of marriage. Worldliness is basically a matter of motives, attitudes, and values. We should not allow the pressures of our society have any negative influence on our beliefs or practices. We need to examine ourselves and see how worldly we are. Do you want to make your marriage better? The way to do this is to become more godly and do it God's way, not world's way. Choose to live free from worldliness and temporal pursuits. Instead bear fruit that will last for eternity.

For the Christian marriage, the choice is clear. Husbands and wives must avoid worldliness in all its forms at all costs. Our goal is to allow the Holy Spirit to take charge of our life and become insensitive to the lusts of the world. Our lifestyle must confirm to that of Jesus, who we are supposed to be imitating.

NOTES

1 H. Murray, "Worldliness," July 2000, https://banneroftruth.org/us/resources/articles/2000/worldliness/
2 John W. Ritenbaugh, "The world, the church, and Laodiceanism," https://www.cgg.org/index.cfm/fuseaction/Library.sr/CT/CGGBOOKLETS/k/452/World-Church-Laodiceanism.htm
3 C. McDowell, "8 important Bible verses about worldliness," https://www.whatchristianswanttoknow.com/8-important-bible-verses-about-worldliness/
4 V. C. Grounds, "Loving the world: rightly or wrongly," *Christianity Today*, vol. 24, no. 007, April 1980, p. 20.
5 M. Prewitt, "The true worldliness of advertising," *Theology Today,* vol. 60, 2003, pp. 384-396.
6 C. Box, "At a time of extraordinary materialism is urgency to avoid hell of worldliness," http://www.spirit-digest.com/Life-after-life

CHAPTER 4

Materialism

"Do not store up for yourselves treasures on earth, where moths and vermin destroy, and where thieves break in and steal. But store up for yourselves treasures in heaven, where moths and vermin do not destroy, and where thieves do not break in and steal" (Matthew 6:19,20).

As mentioned briefly in the previous chapter, materialism is one the greatest enemy of marriages, especially in America. America is a country that guarantees life, liberty, and the pursuit of happiness for its citizens. It prides itself on individualism and its concept of the American dream. Opportunities are everywhere. A person can start from nowhere, work hard, follow the rules, and be successful. The idea that material possessions improve one's personal and social well-being permeates America.

Unfortunately, the American dream is becoming more and more materialistic. Today, there is an endless lists of things that people want: the latest smart phones, luxury cars, designer shoes, and Rolex, etc.[1] Wives or husbands who put a lot of weight on luxury vacations or designer décor may end up not being the perfect match in marriage.

There is even an underlying assumption that there is a direct correlation between wealth and success, wealth and power, wealth and spirituality. Even Christians begin to think that if God loves them He will bless them with a temporal blessing. Most people cannot help but have a materialistic mindset in America.

Through technology, globalization has brought nations together as a village and introduced significant changes in peoples' lifestyles and values. Materialism has become a global phenomenon through modernization and westernization. Most of the developing countries are envious of the Western world and are feeling the pressure of making money and reflecting materialistic tendencies as they develop their economies.

WHAT IS MATERIALISM?

Materialism is part of the American way of life. It defines us, motivates us, and moves our economy more than any other custom. Keeping up with the Jones' is a standard way to describe the goal of the average American. As with all things, materialism has its good and bad points. Some of our basic needs are best met by material things. There is no substitute for a good umbrella on a rainy day. A smart phone provides convenient communication. But some people place a disproportionate high value on things to meet their needs.[2]

Materialism may be defined as a worldview or philosophical system which regards matter as the only reality in the world. Since materialism denies the existence of God, it relies on Darwin's theory of evolution to explain itself and is incompatible with most world religions, including Christianity, Judaism, and Islam. No religion is against material success gained the right way. Religion only opposes the wrong way we can use it.

Materialism is a mindset that desires to make money and spend it on material things, to the neglect of spiritual matters. It is a lifestyle with a high degree of material consumption. It is the act of attaching high value and importance on consumer goods and worldly possessions. It is giving a higher priority to obtaining, maintaining and protecting material objects than developing and enjoying interpersonal relationships. It represents the way people value things such as money, clothes, and social status more than things like knowledge, education, and inventioin. It is foolishly chasing the wind (Ecclesiastes 2:26). It can make or break a marriage. Materialism tends to strain marriages. Married couples who save together and spend together tend to stay together.

Materialism manifests itself in many ways: then obsessive accumulation of unnecessary products, elementary school children having iPhones, teen suicide, depression, the disintegration of the family, divorce, bankruptcy, and despair. Job said that the evil man may accumulate money like dust, with closets jammed full of clothing (Job 27:16, TLB).

Materialism is commonly connected to the notion of culture since it varies substantially across cultures. Countries having a collectivistic culture (such as India) show less prone attitude towards materialistic things than to those following an individualistic culture (such as U.S.).

WHAT CAUSES MATERIALISM

We will consider four major causes of materialism in marriage: our personality, the neighborhood we live in (peer pressure), media, and technology. These are the key sources of materialistic values.

1. Personality: Personality refers to the basic regulatory mechanisms underlying individual behaviors, attitudes, beliefs and values. As far as materialism is concerned, there are two kinds of goals people may have: (1) extrinsic goals which focus on external rewards and are motivated by consumer culture and the opinions of others, (2) intrinsic goals which tend to satisfy inherent psychological needs that all people have. Extrinsic goals tend to diminish the quality of our lives, whereas intrinsic goals promote greater health and more social justice.[3]

2. Influences of Neighborhood: We are often tempted to want and copy what those around us have. We try to "keep up with the Joneses." For example, if we see our neighbor driving luxury cars, we are likely to feel a need to spend money we may not have to project an image of wealth we do not actually possess.

3. Influences of Media: Although wealth plays a major role in being materialistic, the media influences decisions in our everyday lives. Advertising constantly bombards us with the newest gadgets. We must avoid the traps of advertisements because "they want your money." Even children as young as two show preference for advertised brands. In America, holidays (such as Thanksgiving and Christmas) have come to be about shopping and buying new things. To businesses, holidays are about making money and luring consumers to buy their products by lowering their prices.

4. *Influences of Technology:* We live in a marketing-driven and increasingly digital media society. The increase in high tech, digital devices in the areas of household appliances (laptops, microwave ovens, TVs, etc.) has changed the landscape of the American home and family. Digital commerce now allows one to buy and sell goods and services using the Internet and mobile devices. Facebook, Instagram, Twitter, and similar social media are effective instruments of peer influence. These media strongly suggest what you must own to fit in and be considered acceptable. American households will continue to pursue these material goods to satisfy their need for comfort and entertainment.

IMPLICATIONS OF MATERIALISM

Materialists regard possessions and acquisitions as essential to their satisfaction and well-being in life. They judge themselves and others by the amount of possessions accumulated. Materialistic values cause a lot of problems such compulsive and impulsive spending, increased debt, decreased savings, financial turmoil, depression, social anxiety, less satisfaction, vulnerability, insecurity, nongenerosity, and unfulfillment. They can make you lose your perspective, your money, and your morals. They can also lead to unnecessary jealousy and competitiveness, which can cause stress. That is too great a price to pay.

We will consider three of these major problems as they have negative effects on your marriage.

1. *Relationships suffer:* Every kind of relationship falls into these main categories: spouses, friends, parents, siblings, school mates, children, co-workers, etc. All the values that we cherish in relationship - such as love, truth, compassion, and justice - evaporate in a culture of superficiality, which materialism breeds. Money becomes the ultimate arbiter between people. The worth of a person is seen only in terms of how much they earn regardless of the means employed. The love of money becomes the root of evil (1 Timothy 6:10). Not only do our personal relationships suffer, our spiritual relationship with God suffers as well. God blesses

us, we become prosperous, and then we abandon Him. We often make wealth our god, not the true King of heaven.

2. Marriage strained: Materialism causes disaster for a marriage. It likely has harmful effects on a couple regardless of whether the value is shared by both husband and wife. Materialism is harmful in marriage for two main reasons. First, materialism may cause spouses to spend money unwisely, thus creating financial stress in the marriage. Second, materialistic spouses place a high priority on money and are less focused on their marriage relationship.[4]

Materialism is causing human connections as in marriage and friendship to be lost and for the human experience to become less meaningful. It is also linked to less effective communication among married couples, higher levels of negative conflict, lower relationship satisfaction, and less marriage stability.

Studies have shown that the more we love things, the less we want to marry and have kids. There is also an agreement today among experts that money is a key factor in a large percentage of marital conflicts. But the real culprit here is materialism – an underlying assumption that money can buy happiness and success for couples. The quest for more things and the lack of enough money to purchase things desired is a stressor that destroys homes and families, even Christian homes.

3. Debt increases: Materialism can lead to accumulating debt and financial turmoil. It has been associated with credit card misuse. New credit cards come in every day, everyone wanting to lend us money, wanting to help us refinance our homes, pressurizing us to buy more and more. The availability of credit card has eliminated the need to postpone acquisitions and defer gratification until a time when people can pay for what they want with the money they have saved. The proliferation of credit cards and their ease of acquisition ensure that even college students today have opportunities for making credit purchases. Using a credit card can lead to compulsive buying behavior, in which a consumer feels an uncontrollable, a chronic urge to shop and overspend to show their status and affluence. As Will Rogers well said: "Too many people spend money they haven't earned, to buy things they don't want, to impress people they don't like."

Perhaps the best way to end this sections is going over

"15 Things Poor People Do That The Rich Don't:"[5]

1. Poor people watch a lot of TV.
2. Poor people eat fast food.
3. Poor people buy clothes or products that on sale.
4. Poor people wake up later than rich people in their early years.
5. Poor people are really into sports.
6. Poor people don't shower as often as rich people.
7. Poor people blame others for their misfortunes.
8. Poor people have no money saved.
9. Poor people use credit cards or take out a loan for useless things.
10. Poor people tend to have kids earlier in life than rich people.
11. Poor people do not do regular checks with their doctor.
12. Poor people spend money before they get it.
13. Poor people surround themselves with other poor people.
14. Poor people never follow through their ideas or potential.
15. Poor people believe that others should help them reach the top.

OVERCOMING MATERIALISM

If you are convicted that you have developed some materialistic tendencies and you want to cut down, there is hope for you. Here are three suggestions to combat materialism.

1. Expressing Gratitude: The first step in combating materialism is that you must be grateful for the circumstances that brought your wealth and focus on the community that surrounds you. We have many things that some people in other countries can only dream about. We must avoid greed and be satisfied with what we have. Christians who are determined to follow Christ should understand where their treasure really is. We must take time to think of things heavenward. We must be careful not to set our hearts on things that really do not matter. For example, if certain sports on TV begin to adversely affect your family commitments, then pull the plug immediately. As Ali Talib rightly said, "Detachment is not that you should own nothing. But that nothing should own you."

2. *Setting Priorities:* Marital relationships usually fair better when spouses share their goals, priorities, and values. Husbands and wives should sit down and make a number of choices that help in this regard. Jesus said, "Is not life more important than food, and the body more important than clothes?" (Matthew 6:25b). We should transcend the spirit of materialism and remain vigilant against the danger of losing what is more valuable. Spend more meaningful time with your partner. Simplify your life and live a minimalist lifestyle.

Minimize the exposure of your children to media at early age. In other words, limit the amount of time you allow your children to watch TV. Children easily get fascinated towards unrealistic belongings promoted by ads and persuade their parents to purchase them. Unfulfilled requests of children for materialistic things make them unhappy, which may result in conflicting situations in the family. The results of materialism on children is illustrated in Figure 1[6].

3. *Sharing with Others:* In reality, as believers, we are only a trustee of what God has given use. Whatever we possess will not remain with us forever, because we will pass away from this world empty-handed. "After all, we didn't bring any money with us when we came into the world, and we can't carry away a single penny when we die" (1 Timothy 6:7, TLB).

We must learn about materialism from the rich young fool in Luke 12:13-21 and replace selfishness with selflessness. We must learn to share and donate items that we do not really need to those who are less fortunate – the poor, needy, widows, orphans, foreigners, etc. As Billy Graham well said, "God has given us two hands, one to receive with and the other to give with."

CONCLUSION

Materialism is attaching an unhealthy level of importance to worldly possessions. Today, Americans thrive on materialism and we never seem to have enough. They lead the world in the culture of material consumption. Materialism has made Americans selfish, ungrateful, and greedy people. Although materialism itself may not cause marital failure, the commercial debt it can create is "an equal opportunity marriage destroyer." So do all you can to prevent materialism from killing your marriage and keeping you out of heaven.

NOTES

1 S. Khurram, "Is the American dream becoming too materialistic?" https://naturevscivilization.weebly.com/is-the-american-dream-becoming-too-materialistic-by-shanzeh-khurram.html
2 M. L. Richins, "Materialism pathways: the processes that create and perpetuate materialism," *Journal of Consumer Psychology*, vol. 27, no. 4, 2017, pp. 480–499.
3 Lisa Mastny, "Consumerism, values, and what really matters: An Interview with Tim Kasser, https://newdream.org/blog/2011-07-kasser-consumerism-values-and-what-really-matters
4 D. Gibson, "How materialism harms a marriage," October 2011, http://www.foryourmarriage.org/how-materialism-harms-a-marriage/
5 "15 things poor people do that the rich don't," https://www.youtube.com/watch?v=swjSycfB4Gw
6 Vandana and U. Lenka, "A review on the role of media in increasing materialism among children," *Procedia - Social and Behavioral Sciences*, vol. 133, 2014, pp. 456–464.

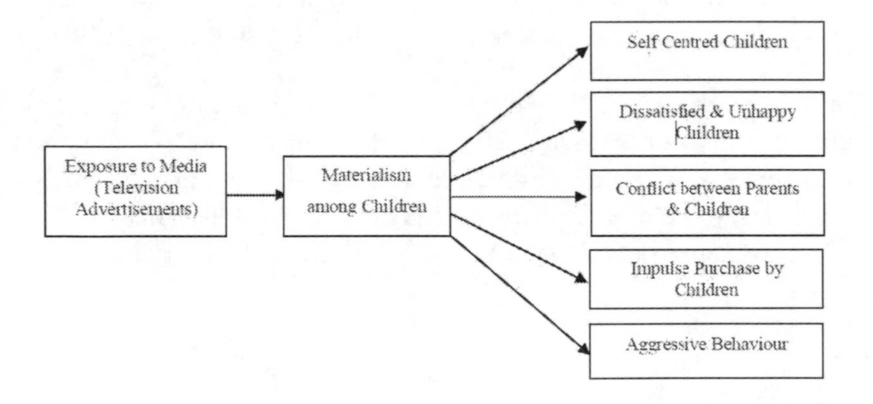

Figure 1 Effects of materialism on children.[6]

CHAPTER 5

The Devil

"We do not wrestle against flesh and blood, but against the rulers, against the authorities, against the cosmic powers over this present darkness, against the spiritual forces of evil in the heavenly places" (Ephesians 6:12)

A lot of things could be working against your marriage: your spouse's mistakes, your own inadequacies, differing personalities, different expectations, a conflict of interest, busyness, sickness, children, in laws, and extended family problems, just to name a few. But none of these are the *real* enemy of your marriage.

Your marriage is under attack whether you realize it or not. Every marriage goes through spiritual warfare. The enemy is real. Your spouse in not your enemy; he or she is your ally. Satan is the enemy of your soul. Satan is working through humans to destroy the fabric of society, including the institution of marriage.

Satan's ultimate aim is to destroy your unity as a couple, diminish your love for your spouse, and ultimately make your marriage fail so that God's purpose for your marriage is not achieved. If Satan fails to destroy a marriage, he will try to weaken it and make it less effective. By this we mean that Satan will prevent the marriage from achieving its intended purpose. He understands that strong families build God's kingdom on earth and raise up a strong next generation.

In this chapter, we will briefly discuss who Satan is, how he operates and what we can do to defeat him.

WHO IS SATAN?

Some Christians believe that the history of Satan is described in the Bible in Isaiah 14:12-15 and Ezekiel 28:12-19. In the Bible, the devil goes by many names including Satan, Lucifer, the Prince of Darkness, ruler of the demons, the god of this world, and adversary of God. The word "Satan" is the English transliteration of a Hebrew word for "adversary." Thus, Satan simply means adversary.

Satan was the greatest of all the angels created by God, but he rebelled against his Creator. Pride originated from his desire to be God instead of a servant of God. Satan pitted his will against God's will and led a revolution among the angels. According to Revelation 12, one third of the angels followed him. As a result, he was cast from heaven and became a fallen angel. God has sealed his ultimate doom (Matthew 25:41).

The fall of Satan shows that angels and human beings can become evil if they so choose. Throughout history, some have disavowed the existence of Satan as a real, personal, spiritual being. Satan himself likes that. But belief in a literal devil and demonic possession remains strong among Pentecostal Christians.

Satan is a wicked being. He strongly opposes every institution of God especially marriage. In our own strength, we are no match for him. We must do what God wants us to do and let God fight our battles for us and give us victory (Deuteronomy 20:4). If we let Him, He will be an enemy to our enemies (Exodus 23:22, Message).

HOW SATAN OPERATES

Satan hates Christians and hates marriages. Therefore, he hates Christian marriages with passion. Satan desires to destroy your marriage. His agenda is clearly stated in John 10:10: "The thief comes only to steal and kill and destroy." We should not be ignorant of his devices (2 Corinthians

2:11). How does Satan destroy marriages? Satan's methods of operation include deception, temptation, instilling doubt and fear, and materialism.

1. Deception: As a deceiver, Satan disguises himself in many forms: as a serpent, a doubter, a lion, etc. Deception is the greatest weapon the prince of darkness relies on. This is the tool Satan used to deceive Eve in the Garden of Eden and fractured the first marriage (Genesis 3). He is crafty and shrewd in his operations. He delights in deception. He seeks to lure individuals and couples into his traps. The devil may deceive you that you are married to the wrong person. When he brings accusation against your spouse, remember that Satan is the "accuser of the brethren" (Revelation 12:10). When your marriage seems not to be doing well, it is tempting to begin to focus on the faults of your spouse. The enemy is good at identifying our weak spots. He is upset at the commitment you made at your wedding, and he is doing everything in his power to make you feel like you made a mistake. He uses emotions and anger to lead us into sin. Through deception and perversion, Satan uses inordinate sexual relations to gratify carnal desires. His grand agenda is to control mankind. He deceives people by saying that "What you don't know cannot kill you." He convinces people that he does not exist. Never believe his pack of lies.

2. Temptation: It is a comfort to know that Satan cannot tempt us through a multitude of channels but can enter our lives through only three gates (1 John 2:16):[1]

- the lust of the flesh,
- the lust of the eyes, or
- the pride of life.

When Satan comes to tempt an individual, he must appeal to one of these basic characteristics of human nature—their carnal capacity, their selfish interests, or their pride. Jesus was tempted in these three areas, yet did not sin (Matthew 4:1-11, Hebrew 4:5). Satan could not reach Job through any of these gates because Job was blameless (Job 2:3).

Because we are prone to put ourselves in situations where we subject ourselves to Satan's attack, we are advised to:

> *Put on the Lord Jesus Christ, and make no provisions for the flesh, to gratify its desires* (Romans 13:14).

We ought to safeguard our minds and hearts so that we do not provide that which Satan can use to produce sin in us.

> *Above all else, guard your affections. For they influence everything else in your life* (Proverbs 4:23, TLB).

3. Doubt and Fear: Like a roaring lion, Satan uses fear to intimidate a believer. He uses fear to instill doubt and unbelief in a believer's mind. He does that in many ways. For example, he makes us anxious about our needs and makes us doubt whether God will provide for those needs and if He even cares about us at all. The fear of not having our needs met is destructive because it threatens our very existence and our marriage. Satan also uses the fear of death to intimidate a believer. He makes us fear the loss of our own life or the life of a loved one. When Satan intimidates us with the fear of death, instead of nursing the idea, we should rebuke him and start praying for the loved one. We must tell him our rights in Christ:

> *No weapon forged against you will prevail* (Isaiah 54:17).
>
> *Whoever touches you touches the apple of his [God's]* eye (Zechariah 2:8)
>
> *Your life is now hidden with Christ in* God (Colossians 3:3).

Since our life is "hidden with Christ in God," Satan cannot touch our life without first touching God. The apostle John wrote, "You, dear children, are from God and have overcome them, because the one who is in you is greater than the one who is in the world" (1 John 4:4).

4. Materialism: The devil can induce a husband or wife to put too much emphasis on pursuing a career, houses, cars, and material wealth. Our society is saturated with materialism, hedonism, and egocentrism. It encourages possessing material things and having a false sense of security. We already covered materialism in Chapter 4.

OVERCOMING THE DEVIL

To counter Satan's attack on marriage, we must understand God's design for marriage and how to oppose Satan's schemes. We overcome the enemy through prayer, sexual intimacy, putting on God's armor, and seeking help when needed.

1. Prayer: Satan desires that we cease communicating with God and one another. Prayer is our lifeline. Marriage is from God, about God, and too many of us neglect God "at our peril." When you pray, you walk in your God-given authority and you have power over your enemy. When things are not going well in your marriage, talk to God about them and ask for His intervention. He will supply the strength and wisdom we need to successfully do battle in our marriages.

As you pray for your spouse, confess your failures. Of course, we do not need to wait till we are in trouble before we pray for our marriages. In spite of what you are going through, you must constantly lean on God. The first and best thing you can do restore or strengthen your marriage is to PRAY.[2]

Pray for your home.
Pray for your mate.
Pray with faith.
Pray with boldness.
Pray with persistence.
Pray with authority.
Pray against the devil.

2. Sexual Intimacy: Husband and wife owe each other sexual intercourse on a regular basis. Paul commanded: "Do not deprive one another.... So that Satan may not tempt you because of your lack of self-control" (1 Corinthians 7:5). Forgive your spouse if he or she has done something wrong. This will keep Satan from getting advantage over you. To safeguard against Satan's temptations, couples must engage in regular, joyful sex. You will not hate your spouse when you pray and have sex together on regular basis.

3. Putting on the Armor: We must constantly be aware of the fact that our warfare is not physical but spiritual and that it takes spiritual weapons to fight it. We must understand our enemy's tactics and use the right weapons to defeat him. That is why we need the armor of God. Paul commanded us to "be strong in the Lord and in the strength of his might" (Ephesians 6:10). This is achieved when husbands and wives "put on the whole armor of God" (v. 11). We are in a daily wrestling match with Satan and his demons (v.12). The battle really belongs to the Lord and we must engage Him. The victory is determined beforehand and the last hour is settled.

In Ephesians 6:10-12, Paul focuses on six indispensable pieces of the armor: a belt, breastplate, shoes, shield, helmet, and sword. They respectively stand for truth, righteousness, the readiness of the gospel of peace, faith, salvation, and the Word of God. Each piece of the armor pertains to a specific spiritual truth related to our identity in Christ. The sword of the Spirit, the Word, is unique because it is the only offensive weapon in the arsenal. Therefore, we need to arm ourselves with the Word.

4. Resisting the Devil: Although Satan can coerce, deceive, and tempt, he cannot override man's free will (James 1:14,15). Each time the devil tempted Jesus, the Lord's resistance was couched in the repetitive refrain: "It is written…" (Matthew 4:4,7,10). The Bible tells us that if we submit to God, then we can resist the devil and he will flee from us (James 4:7).

5. Seeking Help: If you have tried everything and a marital problem still cannot be resolved, you need to seek some outside help. You are not alone in your fight; you are part of the larger community of faith. Involve your pastor, brethren, or someone who is older in the Lord. It is not a sign of weakness to seek counsel. It is easier and less painful to learn from the experience of others. Our plans fail or succeed depending on how informed we are in making them (Proverbs 15:22). Other people who are not directly involved in an issue can look at it more objectively than we can. As the wise man said, "Where there is no guidance, a people falls; but in an abundance of counselors there is safety" (Proverbs 11:14, RSV).

CONCLUSION

Christian marriages are involved in spiritual warfare with a ruthless enemy and the enemy never goes on vacation. His ultimate goal is to weaken your faith and destroy your marriage. This never-ending satanic battle against marriage ought to compel Christian couples to be vigilant and prayerful. We will not have the kind of marriage that God intends us to have unless we are willing to fight for it and pay the price of vigilance. It is incumbent on us as Christians to be aware of the work of the devil who is bent on destroying humanity. Marriage partners must remain on the alert and be sensitive:

"Be sober, be vigilant; because your adversary the devil walks about like a roaring lion, seeking whom he may devour" (1 Peter 5:8).

In order to serve God fully, you need to be free from Satanic bondages and personal bondages. To avoid being useless in our lives and ineffective in our marriage, we need to watch and pray (Mark 13:33). We also need to grow spiritually. Spiritual growth will result in victorious living. It will lead to spiritual power and once you are empowered, you will cease being dominated by circumstances and harassed by the devil.[3]

We have at our disposal Jesus Christ as our greatest ally and the Holy Spirit as our greatest helper. As we avail ourselves of the resources that God has provided, we will enjoy a victorious marriage and our victory over the enemy is guaranteed.

NOTES

1 M. N. O. Sadiku, *Choosing the Best: Living for What Really Matters*. Bloomington, IN: AuthorHouse, 2012.

2 L. Comes, *Six Lies the Devil Uses to Destroy Marriages*. Houston, TX: Lakewood Church, 1988.

3 M. Atunrase, *7 Realities the Devil Doesn't Want You to Know*. Morrisville, PA: Molat Publishers, 2016, p. 68.

CHAPTER 6

Irresponsibility

"All that is necessary for evil to succeed is for good men to do nothing as they must if they believe they can do nothing." -Edmund Burke

Although we have free will to make choices as we deem fit, we are morally responsible for those choices. Failure to accept responsibility for own actions is irresponsibility. It is sad but true that most marriages go through a crisis of irresponsibility at one time or the other.

For a marriage to thrive, you need the ingredients of love, freedom, and responsibility. When two partners are free to disagree, they are free to love. When they are not free, they live in fear, and love dies: "Perfect love drives out fear" (1 John 4:18). Married couples are accountable for their own behavior. In marriage, accountability is answerability. It involves the expectation of account-giving behavior. It is the acknowledgment and assumption of responsibility for actions one takes. It is described as an account-giving relationship between husband and wife. Without responsibility and accountability, freedom is in danger of degenerating into mere arbitrariness.

Marital commitment is morally binding, and suggests that the husband and wife act in such a way that minimizes the any adverse effect on the other spouse. Married couples can be victorious over great odds when they are willing to make the necessary adjustments and take responsibility for their marriage.

Before we discuss about your marital responsibilities and duties, it may be proper to discuss your marital rights and the causes of irresponsible behaviors. Then we can discuss the different levels at which married couples discharge their responsibilities: domestic, financial, and spiritual.

MARITAL RIGHTS

Although marital rights vary from state to state, most states recognize the following spousal rights:[1]

- the ability to open joint bank accounts
- the ability to file joint federal and state tax returns
- the right to receive a family rate on health, car and/or liability insurance
- the right to inherit spouse's property upon death
- the right to sue for spouse's wrongful death
- the right to receive spouse's Social Security, pension, worker's compensation, or disability benefits.

In addition, marriage entitles you to a share of all marital property accrued by your spouse during the marriage. Marriage brings financial, legal, social, and spiritual benefits as well as duties and responsibilities.

One of the key benefits of marriage is that each partner can each do what he or she is best at and reap the benefits of specialization. God has designed us to be free beings and He does not want us enslaved by each other.

There are certain obligations and responsibilities that come with marital rights. We will discuss them in this chapter.

CAUSES OF IRRESPONSIBILITY

The law of responsibility in marriage states that: A husband and wife are responsible *to* each other, but not *for* each other (Galatians 6:2,5). Irresponsibility occurs when the law of responsibility is not obeyed. An irresponsible husband will neglect his responsibility to love his wife. He may become selfish or inconsiderate.

Our first father, Adam, told God, "Eve made me do it." Eve told God, "The serpent made me do it." Blame-shifting, excuse-making, and irresponsibility are built into our DNA.

Although experts disagree as to what exactly constitutes irresponsible behavior, we all can see it when irresponsibility manifests itself. Here are the ways a husband and wife demonstrate irresponsibility at home.

1. Lack of domestic support: Shirking your responsibilities can cause your spouse to feel resentful or create power imbalance in your marriage. Most wives complain that their top source of stress is that their husbands do not want to do their share of chores around the home. When the wife works full time and still ends up doing most of the housework and child care, she resents her husbands' lack of support. If you are endlessly fighting over household responsibilities and roles, your relationship begins to feel adversarial.

2. *Domestic violence*: Violence is designed to overpower an individual and keep the victim in fear of the other. This may take physical, emotional, or sexual abuse.[2] Physical abuse may cause pain, injury, or bodily harm. Emotional abuse or psychological abuse threatens, intimidates, dehumanizes or undermines self-worth of the victim. Sexual abuse is as any attempt to obtain sexual acts or advances. Any form of abuse is improper in the marriage relationship because a marriage cannot thrive when abuse exists, whether it is physical, emotional, or sexual.

3. Addiction: Alcohol and drug addiction can be linked to domestic violence. Addiction affects millions of Americans each year. A couple may be facing serious problems such as alcoholism, neglect, workaholic tendencies, poor communication, etc. Unless the husband and wife take responsibility and change their counterproductive behaviors, they will continue in a vicious cycle. Both the abuser and the abused should seek help. There are treatment centers available all over the U.S. that can help improve your overall quality of life.

4. Infidelity: Infidelity is cheating on a spouse or leaving spouse for another partner. Extramarital sex is a major problem in marriage which can lead to divorce. The solution to infidelity is contentment and self-control. The Bible encourages us to drink from our own well and share our life with only our spouse (Proverbs 5:15). "Don't lust for her beauty.

Don't let her coy glances seduce you. For a prostitute will bring you to poverty, but sleeping with another man's wife will cost you your life. For the woman's jealous husband will be furious, and he will show no mercy when he takes revenge" (Proverbs 6:25,26,34, NLT). If your husband or wife does not satisfy your sexual needs, you should discuss it with them. Leaving her for another woman does not show integrity; it only shows an unwillingness to take responsibility for your own happiness. In addition to contentment, we also need self-control, which is one of the nine fruits of the Spirit (Galatians 5:23). Definitely, self-control serves love, not selfishness.

5. *Wrong Priorities:* Maintaining a proper priority is a constant struggle in many homes. Letting our priorities for our marriage get out of order can lead to acts of irresponsibility. Our priority list in our marriage should go in the following order:[3]

1. God
2. Family – spouse and children
3. Others – job, ministry

These should dictate our levels of commitment.

6. *Financial Debt:* It is well known fact that marital debt can significantly affect a marriage. Not having enough money to adequately support your family can creat great havoc on your emotional and physical well-being. For example, you may lose your job, become pregnant, get sick, become disabled, etc. This can cause your marital debt to increase. It is irresponsible to charge that item on your credit card when you know you will not be able to pay off the bill at the end of the month. Significant debt can make spouses angry and cause depression.[4] This is why the Bible says, "Owe no man anything, but love one another" (Romans 13:8, KJV). It also says, "The rich rule over the poor, and the borrower is servant to the lender" (Proverbs 22:7, NIV).

7. *Bad choices:* Other irresponsible actions include stealing, gambling, having cars or houses you cannot afford, and having too many children you cannot financially support their college education. These bad choices can put a lot of stress on your marriage. It is grossly irresponsible not to cut your cloth according to your size. The majority of children raised by irresponsible parents are negatively affected in terms of their academic performance and social functioning. A spouse who is irresponsible and disorganized (misplacing bills and other important personal documents in the house) can make the life of the other partner difficult and miserable. A spouse's irresponsible behavior is a common cause of marital break ups.

Irresponsibility should not be tolerated in a marriage. Your marriage can be transformed from irresponsible to mutually responsible one. We will now discuss different ways by which married couples discharge their responsibilities: domestic, financial, and spiritual.

DOMESTIC RESPONSIBILITY

Domestic responsibilities are ticking a time bomb in most homes. Sharing household chores ranks high on issues affecting marriages. The general stereotype is that men do not need help and can handle situations on their own, whereas women were perceived as weaker than men. The women's liberation movement has helped change these stereotypes. God never regarded women as second-class citizens. His Word clearly teaches that we are all equally His children and are of equal value (Galatians 3:28). We discuss domestic responsibility in this section along the following concepts: division of labor, understanding, communication, and shared responsibility.

1. Division of Labor: Several decades ago, the division of labor between a husband and wife was clear: he should go to work and earn money, while she should stay at home, cook, clean, and raise the children. This is the traditional model. Things have changed. Today our society has redefined the duties and responsibilities of men and women in society and in the home. More and more women are committed to work outside of the home.

Household work can be categorized into three activities:[5] (1) household maintenance, (2) household chores (e.g., meal preparation, cleaning, outdoor work), (3) childcare. Husband and wife must work together as a team and avoid the 50-50 split. There must be no his work or her work. It is your home, so it is your work. A household will run more smoothly and efficiently if people are allowed to do what they are best at. If you have kids, you should involve them with chores as soon as they are able.

2. *Understanding:* A fair and satisfactory plan for sharing and dividing up household chores begins with mutual understanding. A solid understanding of each other goes a long way in producing happy marriages. To minimize conflict and build healthy lasting relationships, it is important that husband and wife have a clear understanding of how they should relate to each other and what their needs are. Be sensitive to your spouse's natural feelings and tendencies. Rather than fighting against his or her nature, use it to your advantage.

3. *Communication:* You need to talk about these things openly and honestly. As a team, you should feel free to discuss the differences and aim for reaching consensus. You both live in the home. Therefore, you should both have a say. Before you split up chores, agree on what they are: cooking, vacuuming, washing, keeping records or doing the finances, mowing the lawn, taking out the trash, ironing the clothes, cleaning the house, making the bed, etc. Instead of dividing up chores 50-50 or along stereotypical lines, things may work best when you assign the responsibility to the person who is most passionate about that task.

Once you have discussed the responsibilities and expectations, your spouse should be able to hold you accountable for performing your duty. If after discussion, your mate fails to do his share of the household chores, keep in mind that you cannot change your spouse. You should consider hiring some outside help or a housecleaner.

4. *Shared responsibility:* As a couple you are on the same team. You should divide household or domestic responsibilities in a way that honors each other. Thriving couples should work together to manage everyday responsibilities. They must reach a consensus and divide household chores fairly as equal partners. Although chores need to be done, they do not need to cause a problem in your home. A Christian couple must not develop a plan based on what other people think. They must seek a plan that preserves fairness and equity in the way they divide household tasks and responsibilities. This will make both spouses happy.

FINANCIAL RESPONSIBILITY

Money plays a major role in argument and conflicts between married couples. Instead of following the traditional model, it is better that you do what works for your marriage and split your financial responsibilities accordingly.

As the husband, a way to demonstrate financial responsibility to your family is to provide for it. As the head of the home, it is your responsibility to meet the material needs of the family. Paul wrote, "But if anyone does not provide for his own, and especially for those of his household, he has denied the faith, and is worse than an unbeliever" (1 Timothy 5:8).

Since money matters can be emotional and uncomfortable in marriages, it is important to develop strong communication skills that will help openness. Make sure you have both short and long-term goals and you make a plan to reach them. Be willing to address each area of your financial commitmenta: budget, investments, insurance, and credit cards.

SPIRITUAL RESPONSIBILITY

Too often we consider marriage a social custom and ignore its spiritual dimension. Marriage is a permanent, spiritual union of two personalities under God's law. Couples should be willing to take spiritual responsibility for their marriage and do what is necessary to sustain it. A good understanding of your spiritual responsibility or duties, as clearly defined in the Bible, can blend married couples together and produce happy homes.

1. Duties of the Husband: The duties of the husband toward his wife include:[6]

- To leave his family and cleave to his wife (Genesis 2:23,24; Ephesians 5:31).
- To be happy with her (Proverbs 5:18)
- Not to put her away (I Corinthians 7:11).
- To love her as Christ loved the Church (Ephesians 5:25).
- To dwell with her according to knowledge (I Peter 3:7).
- To fulfill her needs (to feed her, provide a shelter for her, etc.)
- To provide for the family (I Timothy 5:8).

As a man, you are a leader, a lover, and a servant of your home. You achieve this by modeling godly character, by praying with your wife, and by looking for ways to encourage her spiritually. Love your wife unconditionally (Ephesians 5:25). Show that you love her in words and in actions. Serve your wife by understanding her needs and making efforts to meet them. Understand her language of love and be her confidant.[7]

2. *Duties of the Wife*: The duties of the wife toward her husband include:[6]

- To honor her husband (Esther 1:20)
- To manage the house well (Proverbs 31:27)
- To be a helper to her husband (Genesis 2:18)
- To respect her husband (Ephesians 5:33)
- To be submissive to his leadership and not usurp authority over him) (Ephesians 5:22; I Timothy 2:12)
- To be gracious, not slanderous, sober-minded, faithful, and patient (1 Timothy 3:11)
- To love her husband and children (Titus 2:4)
- To make herself attractive to him.

Respect, honor, and appreciate your husband. Submit to the leadership of your husband and be willing to meet his needs. As you voluntarily submit to him, you are completing him and helping him fulfill his responsibilities and become the man, the husband, and the leader God intended him to be. You are like a thermostat that controls the emotional climate of the homee. You may need to "speak the truth in love" to him at times. But do not step into Holy Spirit territory. Be his prayer partner, not his Holy Spirit.

CONCLUSION

A healthy marriage results when two people work together to make their marriage work and are determined to tackle the problems that threaten it. As married couple, do not let your domestic responsibilities prevent you from meeting each other's most important emotional needs. A marriage thrives when both the husband and wife are responsible. Your life is your responsibility. Stop blaming others like Adan and Eve. So take responsibility for your own actions.

NOTES

1 K. Otterstrom, "Rights and responsibilities of a married person," https://www.lawyers.com/legal-info/family-law/matrimonial-law/rights-and-responsibilities-of-a-married-person.html
2 "Domestic violence," *Wikipedia*, the free encyclopedia https://en.wikipedia.org/wiki/Domestic_violence
3 M. N. O. Sadiku, *Secrets of Successful Marriages*. Philadelphia, PA: Covenant Publishers, 1991, p. 241.
4 "The emotional effects of marital debt," http://relationshipcounselingcenter.net/emotional-effects-marital-debt/
5 W. Klein, C. Izquierdo, and T. N. Bradbury, "The difference between a happy marriage and miserable one: Chores," March 2015, https://www.theatlantic.com/sexes/archive/2013/03/the-difference-between-a-happy-marriage-and-miserable-one-chores/273615/
6 "Marriage and responsibility," http://www.biblicalfulfillment.org/id61.html
7 J. Karina, "Roles and responsibilities in marriage," http://www.jenniekarina.co.ke/roles-and-responsibilities-in-marriage/

CHAPTER 7

Mixed Faith

"Do not be mismated with unbelievers. For what partnership have righteousness and iniquity? Or what fellowship has light with darkness?" (2 Corinthians 6:14).

The three major influences on our lives are culture, religion, and education. Religion plays a variety of roles in our daily lives. Therefore, mixed faith is a major enemy of marriages because it always causes social and marital frictions. Differences in faith between spouses leads to unnecessary conflicts. I say this partly from experience because my dad was a Christian, while my mom was a Muslim. Both my dad and mom were Muslims originally. When my dad got converted to Christianity in 1965, everyone in the polygamous family was converted except my mom. She remained a Muslim until she died in 2009.

Interfaith (or mixed-faith) marriage (or religious intermarriage) refers to marriage between partners professing different religions.[1] This kind of marriage was uncommon until the modern age. Today, many people marry across religious lines. Mixed-faith marriages are made up of married couples who are from different religious backgrounds. Such marriages are becoming common in the U.S. as they represent close to half of all marriages that began in the past 10 years. Interfaith marriage differs from interracial and inter-ethnic marriage because spouses in an interfaith marriage may share the same race or ethnicity.

The intermarriage of Christians and Muslims, Catholics and Protestants, Jews and Gentiles, Hindus and Mormons, or evangelicals and non-evangelicals is increasing significantly. However, such interfaith marriages usually come with a heavy price. Compared with same-faith unions, interfaith couples tend to be unhappy and mixed-faith marriages often end in tears.

MIXED FAITH MARRIAGE IS FORBIDDEN

The issue of religion can often be the cornerstone of strife in an interfaith union. Shared religious faith is crucial for a successful marriage. If you have fundamentally different spiritual beliefs, this usually presents an additional challenge in your relationship for an entire lifetime. You will be prevented from sharing a big part of your life with your spouse. This negates much of the bonding that usually comes with same-faith marriages.

Most religions strictly prohibit interfaith unions. Mixed-faith unions are forbidden in Islam and Judaism. Most Christian denominations forbid interfaith marriage based on 2 Corinthians 6:14 and Deuteronomy 7:3. Jesus taught that you should value and love Him above all other relationships (Luke 14:26). Our love for Him must be undivided. The apostle Paul commands that Christians must "not be unequally yoked with unbelievers" (2 Corinthians 6:14). Avoiding being "unequally yoked" is excellent biblical advice. Christians should not marry an unbeliever because this violates the believer's union with Christ. We must keep in mind that Christians approach marriage as a covenant, a relationship based on promises and commitment.

For those who embrace a religious outlook on life, faith is a way of life. For those individuals, religion means having a set of values and principles which guide individuals through life. In mixed-faith families, parents come from different faith backgrounds, in any combination between Christian, Hindu, Muslim, and Jew.[2] The diversity of religion may be the source of frequent domestic strife and discord. This could prevent the marriage from fulfilling its intended purpose. Mixed-faith marriage contradicts the principle according to which a man and woman constitute a unity of body and spirit in marriage.[3]

King Solomon made a major self-destructive mistake in marriage. He married multiple foreign women who rejected faith in God alone. As wise and powerful as he was, he could not turn those women to God. In fact, scripture tells us that the women actually turned him away from God. When he became old, his wives turned his heart away after other gods and God was not pleased with him (1 Kings 11:4).

BENEFITS AND CHALLENGES

Perhaps the major benefit of interfaith marriage is that it potentially promotes religious education, tolerance, and accommodation in the society. It also produces religiously tolerant and enlightened children. Marrying someone of another faith tended to improve one's view of that faith. The more one knows people of another faith, the more they like them. With time both partners may decide to merge their two faiths and pursue a way of life that they can both share.

However, an interfaith marriage can pose some major challenges to the couple, to the children, and to extended families. A power usually struggle always exists over which religion is better. Theologians and sociologists contend that interfaith marriages weaken the religious commitment of the individuals forming the unions and the commitment of the offsprings is low.[4] Interfaith marriages are generally less religious than their same-faith counterparts, they attend religious services less often, pray less frequently, and discuss religious matters with their spouses less frequently. Interfaith couples are often overall less satisfied than same-faith couples. When you are in an interfaith marriage, avoiding conflict may require even more effort. Some mixed-faith marriages end in tears and there is evidence that mixed-faith couples have a somewhat higher rate of divorce than do same-faith couples.

Celebrating religious occasions like Hanukkah and Christmas, and Passover and Easter, can be uncomfortable for interfaith couples. Such religious festivals or anniversaries, birthdays, wedding ceremonies, and funerals can present some tensions. It is impractical to raise children in two competing sets of beliefs. Interfaith marriages tend to gravitate to Unitarian Universalism and produce dual-faith children.

STRENGTHENING INTERFAITH MARRIAGE

According to Naomi Schaefer Rile,[5] couples tend to have tensions in their marriages over three things: (1) how to raise their kids, (2) how to spend their free time, and (3) how to spend their money. And religion affects all of those things. 1 Corinthians 7:13-16 is one of the few passages that address interfaith marriages.

Unfortunately, interfaith couples often do not know where to turn to get their problems solved. Your two-religion household can be effective and become a blended family if proper care is taken. Here are some tips that can help you enjoy an interfaith marriage.[6]

1. Communicate: Communication is the process by which you let your spouse know about your feelings, thoughts, problems, etc. It is crucial that you have a thorough, open communication with your spouse on a regular basis. Do not bottle up something you feel is wrong. That will cause resentment and lead to other problems.

You should discuss what you want your child to encounter. Although a child is capable of eventually integrating the two worldviews of their parents, a child cannot be a Muslim and a Catholic at the same time. Parents must decide which way they will raise their child. It is important to make this tough decision early on in the relationship. As long as the married couple have a strong relationship with open communication, they can allow their child to make their own informed choices.[7] There is no universal right way in which "mixed" parents should bring up their "mixed" children.

2. Educate Yourself: (This is still part of communication.) It is critically important to teach yourself about your spouse's faith and culture. The more you know about your spouse, the more you grow in your love for them. Participate and be involved in your spouse's rituals and celebrations. Build bridges of understanding between the two of you.

3. Be Flexible: To make your marriage work, you should be willing to give and take. Be willing to compromise in resolving your marital conflicts. Cherish and enjoy your differences. The earlier you work through your differences the better. Doing so will help you navigate the differences for better rather than for worse.

4. Don't try to Change Your Spouse: If your partner wants to convert and change their faith, let it come from their personal decision Do not force, nag, or give ultimatums. Let love and action do the talking. No one enjoys being criticized for what they believe. Criticizing one another about your faith can be devastating to your relationship. Respect the beliefs and values of your spouse. Do not allow the enemy to use your faiths to tear you apart.

CONCLUSION

Marriage has changed over the years as the society around it has. We are in an era of interfaith marriage. As couples abandon religious boundaries and traditions, religious intermarriages are becoming common. Globalization and migration have greatly contributed to the recent rise of exogamy or interfaith marriages. Although having a close relationship to a perosn of another faith may be enlightening, it is also challenging. Christian or not, a marriage is very hard for any couple to sustain over a lifetime. Statistics show that more than half of the marriages today end up in divorce. If you are in an interfaith marriage, your marriage cannot only survive a faith crisis, but it can thrive as a deeply satisfying friendship. Your marriage can be both successful and happy if you can do what it takes, as recommended above. Other helpful resources include the books by McGowen,[8] Miller,[9] and Seamon.[10]

NOTES

1 R. Cigdem, "Interfaith marriage in comparative erspective," *Acta Orientalia Academiae Scientiarum Hung.,* vol. 68, no. 1, 2015, pp. 59– 86.

2 E. Arweck and E. Nesbitt, "Young people's identity formation in mixed-faith families: Continuity or discontinuity of religious traditions?," *Journal of Contemporary Religion*, vol. 25, no. 1, 2010, pp. 67-87

3 C. Cristellon, "Between sacrament, sin and crime: Mixed marriages and the Roman Church in early modern Europe," *Gender & History*, vol. 29. no. 3, November 2017, pp. 605–621.

4 L. R. Peterson, "Interfaith marriage and religious commitment among Catholics," *Journal of Marriage and the Family*, vol. 48, no. 4, November 1986, pp. 725-735.

5 N. S. Riley, *'Til Faith Do Us Part': How Interfaith Marriage Is Transforming America*. New York: Oxford University Press, 2013.

6 J. Keen, "Avoiding conflict in an interfaith marriage," https://www.kveller.com/article/avoiding-conflict-in-an-interfaith-marriage/

7 E. Arweck and E. Nesbitt, "Religious education in the experience of young people from mixed-faith families," *British Journal of Religious Education*, vol. 33, no. 1, 2011, pp. 31-45.

8 D. McGowan, *In Faith and In Doubt: How Religious Believers and Nonbelievers Can Create Strong Marriages and Loving Families.* New York: AMACOM, 2014.

9 S. K. Miller, *Being Both: Embracing Two Religions in One Interfaith Family.* Boston, MA: Beacon Press Books, 2013.

10 E. B. Seamon, *Interfaith Marriage in America: The Transformation of Religion and Christianity.* New York: Palgrave Macmillan, 2012.

CHAPTER 8

Nagging and Criticism

"*Better to live in a wilderness than with a nagging and hot-tempered wife*" (Proverbs 21:19).

To nag is to bug or make a big deal out of doing something small. Nagging is endless scolding, complaining, and faultfinding. It may also be regarded as constantly criticizing someone. When you complain about or say something over and over again, then it becomes nagging. Nagging can occur in the workplace or at home.

Nagging in a marriage is a common problem. It is poison to a marriage. It is one of the most common relationship complaints couples express. It is never an effective way to communicate your needs or requests. It can be harmful to a relationship and it often produces negative results. It causes vexing and irritation to both partners. It is an enemy of marriages.

Nagging is a form of persistent persuasion that is designed to gain compliance.[1] Nagging is an aggressive, nasty behavior that can stem from unbelief, unmet needs, feeling unheard and unsupported. It is often perceived as criticism and can make others feel inadequate.

Although both men and women nag, nagging is mostly done by women. We have all seen a woman or wife always complaining about things around her home, about her husband, her children, or her job. Women try to get what they want by nagging and criticizing their husband and children. Much of their criticism is well-intentioned. That may be their way of saying I care and demanding to see a change.

King Solomon, the wisest man that ever lived, wrote that is better to sit on a roof and live in a desert than live with a nagging wife (Proverbs 21:9,19). Delilah finally caused Samson's demise by nagging him until he revealed the secret of his strength. Satan may use nagging and criticism to do some havoc in your marriage.

This chapter first considers what is wrong with nagging. It then presents ways of stopping or minimizing nagging and criticism in marriage.

WHAT IS WRONG WITH NAGGING

We all hate nagging. It does not feel like love. Parents are unwittingly, too critical of their children. Parents who nag or overcriticize their children are destroying their fragile self-esteem. Unfortunately, those who nag may not realize that they are nagging. The nagger should understand that there are dangerous consequences for his or her actions. Here are the reasons nagging will not get you what you want in any relationship:[2]

1. Resentment: Because no one likes nagging, nagging will likely generate an angry response from your partner, making them resent you. The more you nag, the less they will respond to your requests.

2. Negativity: When you nag, you are finding fault in your partner. You are implying what your partner is doing is wrong. Who needs nagging, criticism, and negativity? Though one may feel bad after being criticized, later try to find something helpful about the comment. Begin to see the positive side of things.

3. Hostility: Nagging is a form of criticism and it creates hostility in a relationship. Criticism generally can be valid or unjustified. It is difficult, if not impossible, to feel love and acceptance in a nagging or critical environment.

4. Dominance: When you nag your partner, you are treating them like you are dominant and what you say needs to happen at all costs. This is an unhealthy approach to forming a long-lasting and meaningful relationship. Remember, you are a partner, not a dictator.

HOW TO STOP NAGGING AND CRITICISM

It is quite unhealthy for your marriage to be filled with nagging and criticism. If your spouse is nagging, there are various ways to cope. You should take the following actions to minimize nagging and criticism.[3-4]

1. Just Stop Nagging: It takes two people to nag. If one stops, it is mostly likely that the other too will stop nagging. Asking for the same thing over and over again does not work. Although nagging may produce a short-term positive result, you cannot nag someone into permanent change. The sooner you stop, the better chance your relationship will have to grow. The person being nagged should stay calm and disengage, if necessary. It is best not to respond immediate but to wait a little before responding. If the nagger does not stop, you should feel free to walk away and maintain peace.

2. Communicate: Communication is one of the things that can make or break a relationship. It has been well said that all behavior is communication and all communication affects behavior. It is the process of creating meaning between people. As a couple, have you talked about the roles each of you should play in your marriage? Set aside time to be with your spouse for daily conversations. Although nagging is not the best way to communicate, she may find it easier to reach you that way. If you have an issue, bring it up once or twice and talk about it. Talk about the issues and make changes to improve your relationship instead of just being annoyed.

3. Respect Your Spouse: There is no better antidote for criticism and nagging than patient and respectful listening. Focus the nagging or criticism on the *behavior* that needs to change. Pay attention on what your spouse is saying. Make sure that your spouse still feels loved and respected. It is important for your spouse to know that his or her nagging and criticism is harming your spirit.

4. Find a Better Time to Criticize: Criticizing or receiving criticism is very important in any healthy relationship. Criticism is always important for happiness in your relationship and for keeping things in proportion, but it must be done at an appropriate time and place and given in a spirit of humility. It must be clear and constructive. Having constructive criticism or feedback can often be a good thing for a healthy relationship.

It is important to strike a good balance between being excessively critical and being totally uncritical. When criticism is not done properly, it will fail to achieve its intended purpose, even although it is well-intentioned. Learning from constructive criticism or feedback allows you to improve. Criticism allows an opportunity to choose peace over conflict.

5. *Be Understanding:* Through understanding, you can choose to approach your marital problems with patience and compassion. Understand that nobody likes being criticized but, unfortunately it is a fact of life in many marriages. Put yourself in the spouse's shoes. The best way to understand your spouse's viewpoint is to listen to what they are saying. Accept that you are not perfect. Understand where he or she is really coming from. It is unhealthy to keep your emotions bottled up. At an appropriate time, voice your feelings.

6. *Compromise:* Marital relationships function best on give and take. You cannot change someone else, but you can only change yourself. Find common ground. When compromising on something, be sure neither of you are trying to attain something unrealistic. When you show that you are willing to change or help, your partner will be willing to do the same. You may find that spending quality time with her at least once a week may stop the nagging.

7. *Go to counseling:* If after you have tried everything and you cannot fix the problem, you may want to seek outside help. Do not be shy to seek help from a family friend, your pastor, a mentor, or a professional counselor. You should not deal with big problems in marriage all by yourself. Counseling can afford you the privilege to learn new ways to communicate and reach an agreement. It is recommended that you both attend the counseling so that you can work on solving the problems together.

CONCLUSION

Nagging is something that most of us do and may not even realize it. It is not conducive to good relationships, whether it is a father prodding a child or a wife prodding her husband. Pray to God about it. Ask the Holy Spirit to help you change. A nagging spirit, taking the form of domestic criticism, is so ugly that we must keep it out of our homes.

Learn to overlook little, inconsequential things. Don't major on minors. It is important that you find ways to resolve your marital conflicts, stop nagging, and start enjoying your marriage again.

NOTES

1 "Nagging," Wikipedia, the free encyclopedia https://en.wikipedia.org/wiki/Nagging

2 C. Truffo, "Why nagging won't get you what you want," https://www.theravive.com/today/post/why-nagging-wont-get-you-what-you-want-0000237.aspx

3 "Criticism," *Wikipedia*, the free encyclopedia https://en.wikipedia.org/wiki/Criticism

4 "How to deal with criticism," https://www.wikihow.com/Deal-With-Criticism

CHAPTER 9

Infidelity

> *"Flee from sexual immorality. All other sins a person commits are outside the body, but whoever sins sexually, sins against their own body"* (1 Corinthians 6:18).

Infidelity is also known as cheating, adultery, unfaithfulness, or betrayal. It is breaking a promise to remain faithful to a sexual partner. The promise was made in the marriage vows between lovers in the presence of many witnesses. It is being unfaithful to your spouse. Although both women and men commit fidelity, men appear to be more prone to affairs.

Studies show that infidelity takes place in 20 to 25% of all marriages. It is a violation of a couple's sexual exclusivity expectations. This violation results in feelings of rage, betrayal, jealousy, and rivalry. Infidelity is threatening and devastating to a marriage. It is regarded as a betrayal and it destroys the fabric of a relationship which is difficult to repair. The betrayal of the marital exclusivity is done through lies and deception - the two main features of adultery.

Today, infidelity is regarded as the most important reason for divorces. According to Jesus, sexual immorality is the only ground for divorce (Matthew 5:32). Infidelity or sexual immorality is a significant problem that seriously affects a marriage. Therefore, we should see infidelity as an enemy of marriage. Although infidelity can be a problem in dating relationships,[1] in this chapter, we restrict our discussion to how it affects marital relationship.

CAUSES OF INFIDELITY

Infidelity is caused mainly by a number of factors, including lack of satisfaction, workplace temptation, seeking pleasure, pornography, and cybersex.

1. Lack of satisfaction: Men are more likely to engage in extramarital sex if they are unsatisfied sexually in their marriage, while women are more likely to engage in extramarital sex if they are unsatisfied emotionally. For women, relationship dissatisfaction is the number one reason for infidelity, whereas for men it is lack of communication and sexual incompatibility.[2]

2. Workplace: As the number of women in the workforce increases, one would expect the likelihood of infidelity will increase. Workplace interaction between men and women is a leading cause of marital infidelity.[3] The increase in working hours, after work meetings, and a need to work out of town for prolonged periods of time may expose a worker to temptation related infidelity. Married women are less likely to have an affair with co-workers than married men. Although companies cannot ban adultery, they can promote zero tolerance for sexual harassment.

3. Pleasure: Humans are promiscuous and depraved. People get involved in infidelity because of the pleasure, thrill, or excitement associated with sex. Like any other sin, a sexual affair is "sweet." Although affairs can be incredibly sexy, compelling, addictive and sweet, most of them end and the thrill wears off. Reality will set in and infatuation will fade.

4. Pornography: Pornography (or porn) consists of sexually explicit material intended to sexually arouse one who views it. It comes in the form of magazines, movies, TV shows, romantic novels, and the Internet which glamorize sexual affairs. These media promote attractive, near naked models. Today porn is readily available at the click of a button by anyone who has Internet connection.[4]

5. Internet: The use of smart phones and the Internet have provided us with convenient media making it easier to engage in interactions outside of the primary relationship. The proliferation of sex chat rooms and certain dating apps have enabled people to engage in acts of infidelity on and off the Internet. The Internet allows users to hide their identity. Some believe that if a partner engages in cybersex (sexual relationship initiated by online contact) this constitutes infidelity. Cybersex can become addictive and needs to be addressed. Social media makes it easy to exchange sexy pictures with an illicit lover.

Other causes of infidelity include unhappy marriages, lack of love/affection, longing for variety of sexual experiences, revenge, appearance (e.g. unattractive wife), and illness of the faithful partner. Be observant and notice if any of these causes occur in your marriage. Observe if your partner acts suspiciously when phoning or texting. Changes in his/her behavior and appearance may indicate unfaithfulness.

There are many types of infidelity. It can be one-night stands, philandering, or affairs. Each type requires different types of help.

EFFECTS OF INFIDELITY

With infidelity come severe consequences. It affects many people. After the unfaithful partner is found out, feelings of shame, guilt, despair, betrayal, and confusion are evident. The betrayed partner feels disappointed and grieves. Even a single infidelity event can lead to untold harm and conflict.

1. Lack of interest in sex: His sexual interest with you may have waned since he is getting his sexual satisfaction elsewhere. He becomes emotionally distant, withdrawn or depressed. The unfaithful spouse often becomes angry and critical. He changes behavior.

2. Jealousy: Infidelity is a violation of a couple's sexual exclusivity expectations. This violation results in feelings of rage, betrayal, jealousy, and rivalry. Jealousy is a romantic partner's negative reaction to the sexual involvement of the partner with someone else. The manifestation of jealousy differs for men and women. Women feel upset when their husband has invested resources in another woman. Men particularly fear that their mate will have sex with someone else.[5] According to the Bible, "The man who commits adultery is an utter fool, for he destroys himself. For the woman's jealous husband will be furious, and he will show no mercy when he takes revenge" (Proverbs 6:32,34).

3. Punishment: While infidelity is not regarded as a criminal offense in Europe and America, it is criminalized in many countries in Africa, Asia, and the Middle East. Most cultures have ways of inflicting punishment on cheaters. In the US. penalties for adultery range from life imprisonment in Michigan, to a $10 fine in Maryland or class 1 felony in Wisconsin.[2] The wise man said, "Sleeping with another man's wife will cost you your life" (Proverbs 6:26).

4. Disobedience: While adultery is cheating on your spouse, it is also disobeying and sinning against God. It is violating the sixth commandment: "You shall not commit adultery" (Exodus 20:14). "Marriage should be honored by all, and the marriage bed kept pure, for God will judge the adulterer and all the sexually immoral" (Hebrews 13:4).

5. Losses: Some people regard the aftermath of infidelity as worse than losing their partner through death. This is based on the fact that relationships survive after death, but do not always survive after infidelity. The losses experienced in infidelity include:[6]

- Loss of trust
- Loss of loyalty
- Loss of security
- Loss of hopes/dreams
- Loss of faith
- Loss of intimacy and affection
- Loss of self esteem
- Loss of identity
- Loss of feeling special
- Loss of self-respect

Infidelity can impair the trust, security, connection, and intimacy level within couples.[7]

6. Divorce: Divorce may result from infidelity, but infidelity need not result in divorce. We must keep in mind that divorce often creates more problems than it solves. It is more problematic if children are involved. Rather than dissolving the marriage, the affair could be used as a catalyst for positive changes in the marriage.

Other effects of infidelity include family instability, violence, abuse, and health problems.

OVERCOMING INFIDELITY

Just as loving moments are shared together, couples must be prepared to share negative experiences as well. This is part of their commitment to one another: "for better, for worse." Overcoming the devastation of infidelity is not easy, but it can be done. If you suspect that your partner may be cheating, both of you should work as a team and take the following actions.

1. Confess: Since infidelity is a sin against God and your partner, you need to confess it and ask for their forgiveness. The Bible asks us to flee sexual immorality and from any appearance of evil (1 Corinthians 6:18). As part of confession, the unfaithful partner should disclose all of the steps leading up to their affair. The person must be willing to make a major commitment and regain their spouse's trust.[8]

2. Forgive: The infidel or unfaithful person should seek forgiveness of the betrayed spouse. This involves restoration and making a deeper commitment to honor and love their spouse. The betrayed spouse should be willing to forgive the unfaithful spouse. We all make mistakes and we all need forgiveness.

Forgiving each other gives new life to the marriage. It lightens up and is freeing. Love begins to flow again.

3. Address the issues: Statistics shows that women initiate about 75% of all divorces. But most people choose not to divorce but to stay in their marriages after infidelity. Divorce is not the solution, especially when the cheating spouse is remorseful and willing to change. The solution is to find out the issues that caused the infidelity and find ways to address them. True intimacy demands that you talk to each other about your joys and sorrows, the pains and the pleasures. It takes time, effort, and hard work to confront all the issues and mend the marriage.[9]

4. Seek Help: It is expedient to get professional help or to talk to friends or relatives who will be less judgmental. Experienced couple therapists deal with the issue of infidelity on a regular basis in their clinical practices. Get the help you need, both as individuals and as a couple, so that you can bring the situation to an end and enjoy your marriage again. With proper professional counseling, couples stand a good chance of overcoming the trauma of infidelity/an affair.

CONCLUSION

Infidelity is having sexual involvement with someone other than your spouse. It is a behavior that results in the most damage to a marriage. It touches many lives. It can disrupt even so-called happy marriages. If left unchecked, infidelity can cause significant harm to a marriage. The good news is that you can recover your marriage, but it takes time and teamwork to heal from infidelity.

If your marriage is in need of restoration right now, pray that God will intervene, guide, and give you wisdom. Remove the option of divorce, forgive, and reconcile. Do not rush into any decisive action. God hates divorce (Malachi 2:16) and loves those who obey Him by not divorcing their spouse. More information on infidelity can be found in Lusterman[10] and Brown.[11]

NOTES

1 R. D. McAnulty and J. M. Brineman, "Infidelity in dating relationships," *Annual Review of Sex Research*, vol. 18, no.1, 2007, pp. 94-114.
2 "Infidelity," *Wikipedia*, the free encyclopedia https://en.wikipedia.org/wiki/Infidelity
3 M. Kuroki, "Opposite-sex coworkers and marital infidelity," *Economics Letters*, vol. 118, 2013, pp. 71–73.
4 "Pornography," https://www.psychologytoday.com/us/basics/pornography
5 H. A. K. Groothof, P. Dijkstra, and D. P. H. Barelds, "Sex differences in jealousy: The case of Internet infidelity," *Journal of Social and Personal Relationships*, vol. 26, no. 8, 2009, pp. 1119–1129.
6 "Coping with Infidelity: A life effectiveness guide," http://www.counsellingconnection.com/wp-content/uploads/2011/04/COPING-WITH-INFIDELITY.pdf
7 K. M. Hertlein, J. L. Wetchler, and F. P. Piercy, "Infidelity," *Journal of Couple & Relationship Therapy*, vol. 4, no. 2-3, 2005, pp. 5-16.

8 Boston Counseling Therapy, "Adultery counseling: infidelity facts, and how to overcome," http://thriveboston.com/counseling/adultery-counseling-information-on-adultery-and-how-to-overcome-its-effects/
9 M. Weiner-Davis, "10 things you must know about infidelity and cheating," https://www.huffingtonpost.com/michele-weinerdavis/10-things-you-must-know-a_b_7247708.html
10 D. Lusterman, *Infidelity: A Survival Guide*. Oakland, CA: New Harbinger Publications, 1998.
11 E. M. Brown, *Patterns of Infidelity and their Treatment*. Bristol, PA: Taylor & Francis, 1991.

CHAPTER 10

Unforgiveness

"Be tolerant of one another and forgive each other if anyone has a complaint against another. Just as the Lord has forgiven you, you also should forgive" (Colossians 3:13).

Unforgiveness is having a grudge against someone who has offended you. It is not having the willing heart to forgive others. One cannot forgive unless unforgiveness has occurred. Unforgiveness is a reaction to a transgression. It is a "cold" emotion involving resentment, bitterness, anger, fear, and perhaps hatred.[1]

Unforgiving people are their own worst enemy. Negativity cancels out creativity. No good can come out of unforgiveness. It is an enemy of your marriage. It comes in many forms and can manifest as a critical spirit, or bitterness, or wrath, or even just irritation. Unforgiveness is the root of many things that separate us from God and others. Some regard it as a curse.[2]

Consider the following quotes on unforgiveness:

"One of the most devastating symptoms of pride is the unwillingness to forgive." — Wayne Gerard Trotman

"Forgiveness is the virtue of the courageous, the response of the forgiven, the mercy of the just." — Ron Brackin

"To violate the law of love is to live in un-forgiveness." — Sunday Adelaja

"Someone once said that unforgiveness is like a poison you drink while hoping for someone else to die." — Jennifer Heng

"When boiled down to its essence, unforgiveness is hatred." — John R. Rice

CAUSES OF UNFORGIVENESS

As long as we live in this imperfect world, interacting with imperfect people, you are bound to offend someone or someone is bound to offend you. When someone offends you, you have a choice to either forgive or not to forgive them. Unforgiveness occurs when you choose not to forgive and be kind to the person who has offended you. It is either doing nothing about the hurt or attemping to punish the transgressor somehow.

The causes of unforgiveness include the following:

1. The sins and failures of others makes us feel deserving of anger.

2. All the other person's wrongs against us become like a loaded gun that we carry around.

3. If you are finding it hard to forgive someone, you are likely bottling up anger.

4. It is tempting to usurp God's position and make yourself judge, jury, and executioner of the person who wronged you.

5. The cost of not allowing the victim off the hook may be a lifetime of unhappiness and bitterness.

6. Unforgiveness catches us in a snare of Satan.

CONSEQUENCES OF UNFORGIVENESS

The consequences of unforgiveness are deadly and detrimental. These include the following.

1. *Festers Bitterness:* Unforgiveness does not promote justice. If left untreated, unforgiveness festers into bitterness and resentment, which a like poison or a cancer and can make you physically sick. Randle Lowrance said, "Bitterness is believing God got it wrong, worry is believing God will get it right, and unforgiveness is believing that you are right even after God says you are wrong." Esau held unforgiveness against his brother Jacob. He became embittered against Jacob and was planning to kill him (Genesis 27:41).

2. *Hurts Relationship:* Unforgiveness blocks love flow in relationships. Unforgiveness, resentment, and bitterness are spiritual maladies that keep many people from living a Spirit-filled life. They affect our relationships and turn our allies (spouse, children, parents, relatives, friends, co-workers, acquitanainces, etc.) into our enemies. They can make us cynical, unable to trust, and unable to maintain close relationships. They give Satan a foothold in our lives.

3. *Causes Damage*: Medical practioners have observed that there is a relationship between forgiveness and health. We suffer alone and in silence when we refuse to allow ourselves to experience God's complete forgiveness. We live in a dangerous cycle of unforgiveness. Unforgiveness can cause spiritual and physical damage. It hurts the one who refuses to forgive. Serious diseases can develop as a result of the poison of unforgiveness a person carries around with them. These may include health challenges such as heart problems, high blood pressure, etc. "They increase the 'bad' (LDL) cholesterol levels and decrease 'good' (HDL) cholesterol levels. Unforgiveness can decrease the blood flow through the coronary arteries that supply the heart itself."[3]

4. *Hinders Prayer*: Unforgiveness prevents us from coming into God's presence. It prevents God from forgiving us (Matthew 18:35). God does not want us and our gifts in His presence if we harbor unforgiveness (Matthew 5:24). I do not care how much you know how to pray or what you are going through, your prayer life is affected negatively by unforgiveness. You only deceive yourself. Your prayer simply won't work in an atmosphere of unforgiveness (Psalm 66:18). God will deal with those who hurt us if we forgive and let Him avenge for us. Vengeance belongs to God (Romans 12:19).

Unforgiveness not only hinders prayers, it is one of the major blocks to receiving deliverance and healing from the Lord.

DEALING WITH UNFORGIVENESS

Forgiving is the way to deal with unforgiveness. Unforgiveness is a common marital problem, and forgiveness is the solution. Needless to say that forgiveness is a much better alternative than harboring unforgiveness. Extending forgiveness to those who have hurt us will actually benefit us more than it will benefit them.

Forgiveness is simply letting go and building the confidence necessary to experience a healthy life. It is an active process in which you make a conscious decision to let go of negative feelings whether the person deserves it or not.[4] It is a task that requires a transition from negative emotions to positive ones. You will never be able to forgive if you wait until you feel like doing so. Your feelings will need time to catch up with your decision to forgive.

Forgiveness is a demonstration of overcoming evil with good and the divine institution for dealing with injustice. It has the power to heal emotional wounds and restore human relationships.[5] The goal of forgiveness is reconciliation with those who offended you, rather than revenge.

1. *God Demands Forgiveness:* In Matthew 18:21-35, Jesus told a parable about the unmerciful servant, who was forgiven much by the king but then refused to forgive the small debt of another man owed him. Because of this, the king rescinded his prior forgiveness. Jesus concluded by saying, "This is how my heavenly Father will treat each of you unless you forgive your brother or sister from your heart" (Matthew 18:35). Jesus also taught His disciples that unforgiveness is unforgivable (Matthew 6:14). He told Peter that he should forgive indefinitely (Matthew 18:21,22).

Forgiving those who have offended us is never going to be easy because it is a God-like trait to be forgiving. As Alexander Pope said, "To err is human, to forgive, divine." But whenever God asks us to do something, it is always for our benefit. He has given each one of us the ability to forgive those who wrong us. It is up to us to use that ability. Forgiveness is a choice we must make. It is consciously choosing to offer compassion and empathy to the person who has wronged us. It takes a major effort of the will to forgive. When we choose to forgive someone, we release the person from his indebtedness to us. We have been given much through forgiveness, and much is expected from us (Luke 12:48). As Ruth Bell Graham said, "A happy marriage is the union of two good forgivers."

2. *Be quick to forgive:* Someone has said "The first to apologize is the bravest. The first to forgive is the strongest. The first to forget is the happiest." God forgives our sins, puts them as far as the east is from the west, and remembers them no more (Psalm 103:12). In the same way, we His children must learn how to forgive and forget. We are to forgive as soon as possible. Joseph readily forgave his brothers because he knew that God turned their evil plan to good (Genesis 50:20). If God puts it in your mind to forgive someone, be ready to do it. You can do all things through Christ who strengthens you (Philippians 4:13).

3. *Love Your Enemy*: Do not seek revenge or bear a grudge (Leviticus 19:18). Rather, we are to love our enemies (Matthew 5:44). Although Jesus was tempted in all the ways we are tempted, He forgave. On the cross, He prayed for His enemies: "Father, forgive them. They know not what they do" (Luke 23:34).[6]

4. *Pray:* Ask the Lord to give you the power to forgive people who have offended you. "Forgive as the Lord has forgiven you" (Colossians 3:13). Like God has done toward us, we need to extend kindness and mercy to others and treat them better than they deserve. Ask God to cleanse and heal you from all of the bitterness, anger and resentment from these hurts and pains.

5. *Repent*: Unforgiveness is a sin. Repent of it and allow God to give you that the grace that will empowering you to forgive those that have injured you. When a person genuinely forgives from the heart, they are able to find a sense of peace.

CONCLUSION

As Martin Luther King Jr. said, "Forgiveness is not an occasional act, it is a constant attitude." Forgiveness is the choice we make every day, not based on feelings. It is based on the fact that no spouse is perfect. It may seem unnatural to forgive because fairness demands that people should pay for their wrong doing. But forgiving is love's power to break nature's rule.[6]

Unconditional forgiveness is the ideal; that involves letting go completely of victim. Wise people forgive but do not forget. Do not let unforgiveness control you. Make forgiveness an ally of your marriage. A marriage that practices forgiveness is destined to last and be happy.[8]

NOTES

1. E. Worthington and N. G. Wade, "The psychology of unforgiveness and forgiveness and implications for clinical practice," *Journal of Social and Clinical Psychology*, vol. 18, no. 4, 1999, pp. 385-418.
2. D. Eells, *The Curse of Unforgiveness*. UBM Books, 2014.
3. "The harmful effects of unforgiveness" https://whatyourfutureholds.wordpress.com/2009/01/29/the-harmful-effects-of-unforgiveness-benefits-of-forgiving-are-worth-reading-about/
4. "Forgiveness: Your health depends on it," https://www.hopkinsmedicine.org/health/healthy_aging/healthy_connections/forgiveness-your-health-depends-on-it
5. Z. Szablowinski, "Between forgiveness and unforgiveness," *The Heythrop Journal*, 2010, pp. 471–482.
6. E. Worthington et al., "Interpersonal forgiveness as an example of loving one's enemies," *Journal of Psychology and Theology*, vol. 34, no. 1, 2006, pp. 32-42.
7. L. B. Smedes, *Forgive and Forget*. New York: Harper & Row, 1984, p. xii.
8. T. Ikomi, *Forgiveness Discipleship: Forgiveness in the Family*. New York: Triumph Publishing, 2015.

CHAPTER 11

Bitterness and Resentment

> "*A foolish son is a grief to his father and bitterness to her who bore him*" (Proverbs 17:25, RSV).

Bitterness and resentment often go together and are the result of unresolved anger. While bitterness is a feeling of deep anger and resentment, resentment is often regarded to be synonymous with anger, spite, and other similar emotions. Both of these outcomes are usually expressed outwardly against those around us, especially the ones we love the most.[1]

When you are offended by someone and allow the hurt to germinate in your heart, bitterness and resentment will take root. Feelings of bitterness and resentment are universal. We all experience them at some point in our lives, regardless of our age, race, sex, economic status, etc. Since they are the source of problems in many marriages, they are an enemy of your marriage. In fact, they are the most toxic of all emotions in marriage.

Parents are often the most common victims of bitterness and resentment because they are blamed for most of our failures. Some feel that their parents destroyed their self-esteem, undermined their confidence, and prevented them from achieving anything worthwhile. Research shows that criminals are great resenters of their parents.[2]

Bitterness is basically being resentful against someone or something that has offended us. As Gregory Popcak well said, "Bitterness is unforgiveness fermented." It usually starts out in a small way. A person who is bitter is often resentful, cold, and unpleasant to be around. Bitterness is a depressant. Bitter people are usually unhappy and depressed, hateful, cruel, mean, and hard to deal with. They are miserable and they tend to make others miserable. Listen to the following quotes on bitterness and resentment:

"Bitterness is like cancer. It eats upon the host. But anger is like fire. It burns it all clean." — Maya Angelous

"Bitterness imprisons life; love releases it." – Harry E. Fosdick

"As I walked out the door toward the gate that would lead to my freedom, I knew if I didn't leave my bitterness and hatred behind, I'd still be in prison." — Nelson Mandela

"Resentments are like swallowing poison and expecting the other people to die." — Malachy McCourt

"Harboring resentment is like slapping yourself and then expecting the other person to feel the pain." Mark Sichel

"Anger, resentment and jealousy doesn't change the heart of others-- it only changes yours." — Shannon L. Alder

"As smoking is to the lungs, so is resentment to the soul; even one puff is bad for you." — Elizabeth Gilbert

CAUSES OF BITTERNESS AND RESENTMENT

These are the common causes of bitterness and resentment in marriage.

1. *Unfair Treatment*: Bitterness can develop from feeling betrayed, marginalized, or taken advantage of. Resentment is the persistent feeling that one is being treated unfairly. This may be due to painful experiences from home, church or workplace. It may also be caused by a relationship breakup, loss of a job, unfair treatment, discrimination, prejudice, etc. Resentment may also be racially motivated. Racial resentment (or symbolic racism) may encompass anger, bitterness, or concern related to one racial group.[3] People who go through life demanding their own way

often feel bitter and resentful towards God and others when they feel overlooked or shortchanged.[4]

After losing her husband and two sons, Naomi, the mother-in-law of Ruth, said, "Things are far more bitter for me than for you, because the LORD himself has caused me to suffer" (Ruth 1:21). Naomi blamed God for her loss and for making her life bitter. She felt God had not been fair to her. She did not realize that God had a plan working behind the scenes. God knew what He was doing. If Naomi's son had not died, Ruth would not have been free to marry Boaz and given birth Obed, the grandfather of David, from whose lineage comes the Messiah Jesus Christ.[5] The Bible says that all things work together for good for those who love God (Romans 8:28).

Like Naomi, the loss of loved ones can create bitterness. I went through that experience when I lost my first wife. She was a wife of my dream and I was embittered for losing her to breast cancer.

2. *Unresolved Anger*: Bitterness is unresolved, unforgiven anger. Heath Lambert said, "Bitterness is the long term anger that accrues in your life when you refuse to forgive someone who has sinned against you."[6] The moment you start hating a person, you become that person's slave.

3. *Unforgiveness*: Bitterness can often be traced to unforgiveness. An unwillingness to forgive others is usually at the very heart of bitterness.

4. *A Root*: Bitterness is a root, and roots are not always visible on the surface (Hebrews 12:15). Before there is a root there is a seed. The seed is planted when someone does you wrong and the plant grows. Bitterness is a hidden element that lies under the surface, invisible to the eyes. That makes it harder to identify and expose. Demons thrive on bitterness and resentment.[7] As a Latin proverb says, "He who goes angry to bed has the devil for a bedfellow."

The sin of bitterness can do the following:[8]

- It can rob you of your peace and joy.
- It is an open door for Satan to control your life.
- It can lead to the loss of good friends.

- It can hurt or destroy you relationship with your family, your wife and can even lead to the breakup of your home.
- It makes peace and harmony impossible.
- There can be no true biblical love where it exists.
- It destroys any true relationship with the Lord and will keep you from growing in the Lord.
- It will defeat you and ruin your life and the lives of those around you.

This is how you know that you spouse resents you:[9]

1. Withholding sex
2. Lack of affection
3. Increased number and intensity of fights
4. Sadness
5. Feelings of helplessness and hopelessness
6. Reluctance to celebrate milestones
7. Withdrawal from the relationship

EFFECTS OF BITTERNESS AND RESENTMENT IN YOUR MARRIAGE

Bitterness and resentment affect your relationships, health, well-being, and career. They put you in a constant "complaining and murmuring mode." When you are bitter, you tend to blame someone else. Bitterness affects us physically, emotionally, socially, and spiritually. It hardens your heart. It is destructive. Bitterness can cause people to begin seeing the world through a negative lens. This negative way of seeing the world and people is isolating. Therefore, we must not allow "bitter roots" to grow in our hearts and cause us to fall short of the grace of God (Hebrews 12:15).

OVERCOMING BITTERNESS AND RESENTMENT

For sure, you cannot beat bitterness with becoming more bitter or beat resentment by being more resentful. You owe it to yourself to seek to overcome bitterness by taking the following actions.

1. *Forgive*: First and foremost, you must learn to forgive and let go. The antidote to bitterness and resentment is forgiveness. The solution to bitterness and resent may mean untangling webs that go back for years. It may entail forgiving those who have wronged us. Our lack of forgiveness is why we choose to hold onto bitterness. Forgiveness is a great psychological release, while unforgiveness is a hell-bent sin. It is impossible to go through life without somebody offending us. We must learn to forgive them and move on with our life.

If we refuse to forgive those who sin against us, God will not forgive us (Matthew 6:15). As Christians, remember that we are forgiven people. As we receive forgiveness, we ought to forgive others too.

Do not listen to those who claim that forgiving is a sign of weakness. Forgiving others is a courageous act that reflects the forgiving, kind, and compassionate attributes of God.

2. *Be Kind*: To release yourself from bitterness, cultivate loving kindness towards yourself and others. If the bitterness and resentful are due to someone, take the initiative to reconcile. God wants us to be peacemakers (Matthew 5:9). Return love for hurt. Life is too short to hold yourself and others in prison. "Be kind to each other, tenderhearted, forgiving one another, just as God has forgiven you because you belong to Christ" (Ephesians 4:32, TLB). Husbands are asked to love their wives and not be bitter against them (Colossians 3:19). Romans 12:18 says, "If it is possible, as far as it depends on you, live at peace with everyone."

3. *Communicate*: Being able to communicate your feelings is helpful in overcoming bitterness and resentment. The communication must be fair to both parties in order to be effective. People often resolve their bitterness and resentment through communication. Feel free to communicate your request or even a boundary without blame. Let your talk be coupled with kindness, love and honesty. The Bible says that we should tell the truth in love (Ephesians 4:15). Your goal is to be able to reach some agreement that will help dissolve your bitterness and resentment and move you closer to one another.

4. *Seek Help*: If you are still having trouble with bitterness and resentment, I strongly recommend that you seek help of your friends,

loved ones, or a counsellor. They may help you process your feelings and shift your perspective. Take responsibility for your actions.

In the same way, the following ways will prevent resentment from destroying your marriage:[10]

1. Acknowledge your feelings and practice being vulnerable in small steps.
2. Be honest and communicate about key issues in your relationship.
3. Take responsibility for your part in the conflict or dispute.
4. Apologize to your partner when appropriate.
5. Practice forgiveness.
6. Show empathy to your partner.
7. Pray earnestly for your spouse.
8. Express thoughts, feelings and wishes in a respectful way.
9. Make a commitment to practice endurance and patience.
10. Replace resentment with compassion and acceptance.

Focus on making your marriage a priority. Spend time together. Boost up your physical affection and sex because physical contact reduces pain and causes a calming sensation. Sex is physically connecting and has a way of softening your minds toward each other.

CONCLUSION

A Christian should not be bitter and resentful because bitterness is a rejection of God's sovereignty, plan, and purpose for our lives (1 Samuel 1:10, Romans 8:28). Resentment is a sin against God and the individual. Because of their destructive nature, bitterness and resentment should be avoided at all costs. They are toxic or poisonous to your marriage. If permitted, they will destroy the relationships with your spouse, children, friends, and even with God. Take prompt and decisive action against bitterness and resentment.

NOTES

1 R. W. Kahle, "Bitterness and resentment," http://www.kindredspiritministries.org/resources/17345.pdf
2 D. Theodore, "The use of resentment," *Psychology Today, vol. 28,* March 1995, pp. 30-32.
3 F. L. Samson, " Racial resentment and smoking," *Social Science & Medicine,* vol. 126, 2015, pp. 164-168.
4 J. I. Wilson, *How to be Free from Bitterness.* Moscow, ID: Canon Press, 2004.
5 "The heart of bitterness," http://biblicalcounselingcoalition.org/2014/02/21/the-heart-of-bitterness/
6 Heath Lambert, "Overcoming bitterness (a transcript) https://biblicalcounseling.com/2016/12/overcoming-bitterness-transcript/
7 "Root of Bitterness." http://www.greatbiblestudy.com/bitterness.php
8 "Bitterness," http://bible-truth.org/msg162.html
9 L. Howard, "7 signs your partner resents you," https://www.bustle.com/articles/161065-7-signs-your-partner-resents-you
10 T. Gaspard, "Is resentment ruining your marriage?" https://www.huffingtonpost.com/terry-gaspard-msw-licsw/is-resentment-ruining-your-marriage_b_5531600.html

CHAPTER 12

Overcommitment

"Nobody on his deathbed ever said, 'I wish I had spent more time on my job.'" – Paul Tsongas

Overcommitment is plaguing our society and our marriage is unfortunately the first casualty. Experts have cited overcommitment as one of the top five relationship killers. Dr. James Dobson, a noted psychologist in California, said: "The most dangerous threat to family life is one seldom mentioned. We can talk about alcoholism, drug abuse or infidelity, but a more common threat is the simple matter of overcommitment." He continues, "I'm talking about the husband and wife who are too exhausted to take walks together, understand one another, meet each other's needs, have time for play, have time for children, have time for devotions. The husband often moonlights to maintain some standard of living; the wife works and tries to oversee the home; everyone is on the brink of exhaustion."[1]

Overcommitment is obliging to do more than one is capable of. It may be regarded as a set of attitudes, behaviors and motions that reflect a person's excessive striving for approval and appreciation. It is the inability to withdraw from obligations at work.[2] Overcommitted individuals are doing way too much, trying to handle a hundred things at once. They are very ambitious and tend to exaggerate their efforts while at the same time overtax their resources.

You may be a superman or a high-achieving woman, you are probably not be a good material for marriage. Overcommitment, time pressure, is an enemy of your marriage.

CAUSES OF OVERCOMMITMENT

Just about any adult you talk to today struggles with busyness and stress. It may be due to involvement in church activities, being involved in their children's extracurricular activities, serving as organization's board members, taking some college classes, busyness at work, invitation to attend an event, shopping, maintaining a supper clean house, taking charge of health through exercising, visiting relatives, etc. Overcommitment, overpromising, overextending, and overdoing do not help us live a balanced life. Some of the causes of overcommitment include busyness, lack of goals and priorities, and pleasing others.

1. *Busyness:* Sometimes life can be very busy due to circumstances outside of our control. It is a fact that we are too busy. Your to-do list has exploded. You find yourself overbooked for several activities. You are overcommitted and overwhelmed.

You may even find yourself putting in extra hours at night when you would normally be sleeping.

2. *Lack of goals and priorities:* It is easy to get distracted and follow the crowd when we do not have personal goals and priorities to achieve the goals. Someone has said that goals are the oxygen to our dreams. They are the first steps to every journey we take. If you don't plan your life, others will decide for you.

3. *Pleasing others*: We seek to gain other people's approval. We find it hard to say no to their requests. Overcommited people excessively strive for approval and appreciation. But a people-pleasing attitude can run havoc in a marriage. Without knowing it, spouses let their marriage suffer at the expense of doing favors for others.

EFFECTS OF OVERCOMMITMENT

Overcommiment is not good for your marriage. It can lead to loss of credibility/integrity, stress, health-related problems, and a bad marriage.

1. *Loss of Credibility:* We like to be men and women of integrity. Whenever you fail to live to up to your commitments, it hurts your credibility and the level of trust others have in you. When you say yes instead of no, it is difficult to be trusted to fulfill your commitments. Your track record for fulfilling your commitments is critical to building your credibility.[3]

2. *Stress*: Stress and burnout are expected outcomes of overcommitment to work overtime. Work-related stress is associated with an increased risk for cardiovascular disease. Overcommitted persons often judge their work situations as more demanding than less committed persons. They are driven by their high need for approval and appreciation, thereby precipitating stress and exhaustion in the long run. The demands they place upon themselves may lead to increased levels of stress.[4] To avoid stress, being overwhelmed and overcommitted should not be a normal part of your professional life.

3. *Health problems*: Overcommitment can lead to depression, diabetes, sleep problems, poor blood sugar control, inflammatory disease, and cardiovascular disease. It can lead to the mental state of vital exhaustion, which is characterized by unusual fatigue, irritability, and demoralization and an established predictor of heart disease. It may also cause sleep problems such as sleep disturbances, insomnia, and poor sleep quality.

4. *Bad marriage*: Overcommiment is not good for your marriage. It makes you sacrifice things that are irreplaceable. These include values and relationsips – between spouses, parents/children, friends, etc. Overcommitment does not provide time for husband and wife to adequately communicate with each other, pray together, enjoy a sexual relationship, or raise kids together. Overcommitted individuals do not live a balanced life and cannot give to their spouse and children what they need.

AVOIDING OVERCOMMITMENT

While it is good to have a passion and a dream, it should be kept in balance with other valuable components of your life. Learning to break the pattern of overcommitment requires discipline and patience. Realizing that time is a finite commodity, you must keep your life in balance. The following tips will help you achieve this and avoid overcommitment.

1. *Prioritize*: We must apply wisdom on how we spend our precious time. We must prioritize our commitments. Here are three levels of commitment in order of importance:[5]

(1) Commitment to God

(2) Commitment to family

(3) Commitment to others, work, ministry or vocation

This indicates that you need to spend more time with God and your partner and kids. A lot of people mix up the order and run into trouble. Being able to set priorities and allocate time appropriately are critical time management skills we must develop.

Select what is more important and focus on actitives that support your priorities. Be realistic and avoid last-minute commitments. Delegate what you can. Learn from past experience to balance your commitments in the future. It is very difficult if not impossible to have it all — the career, the family, the social life, the spiritual life, etc. You need to figure out what you value most, and allocate your time and money to pursing them.

2. *Learn to say no:* Once you know what your priorities are, learn to say no to other commitments. Learning to say no may be difficult, but we must learn this important lesson. Before you say yes to an opportunity to serve, count the cost and ask yourself if the commitment is going to cut into your time with God and your family. For every commitment you make, you put your integrity on the line. Turn down new opportunities to serve if they would stretch you too thin.

3. *Rest more*: Sleep rejuvenates our body and reduces stress. Sleep is important for various activities of brain function such as cognition,

concentration, productivity, and performance. Each of these activities is negatively impacted by sleep deprivation.[6] Failure to reserve some time for enough rest (as Jesus did) is risking even the good things we are committing ourselves to.

CONCLUSION

The breathless lifestyle that most Americans engage in is unacceptable. It is not healthy for your marriage. Make every effort to resist the temptation of overcommitment. For the sake of your marriage and family, you should not overcommit yourself. Don't let overcommiment crowd out your valued relationships. Instead, thehusband and wife should be fully committed to what God has purposed for their marriage.

NOTES

1 B. Barlow, "Overcommitment labeled no. 1 thtreat to marrages," https://www.deseretnews.com/article/40211/OVERCOMMITMENT-LABELED-NO-1-THREAT-TO-MARRIAGES.html

2 D. Preckel et al., "Overcommitment to work is associated with vital exhaustion," *International Archives of Occupational and Environmental Health*, vol. 78, no. 2, March 2005, pp. 117–122.

3 "Two keys to avoid over-commitment," http://www.andersonleadershipsolutions.com/two-keys-to-avoiding-over-commitment/

4 Å. B. Rennesund and P. Ø. Saksvik, "Work performance norms and organizational efficacy as cross-level effects on the relationship between individual perceptions of self-efficacy, overcommitment, and work-related stress," *European Journal of Work and Organizational Psychology*, vol. 19, no. 6, 2010, pp. 629-653.

5 M. N. O. Sadiku, *Secrets of Successful Marriages*. Philadelphia, PA: Covenant Publishers, 1991, p. 241.

6 J. Leech, "10 reasons why good sleep is important," https://www.healthline.com/nutrition/10-reasons-why-good-sleep-is-important#section1

CONCLUSION

You can have a solid, dynamite, happy marriage if you are willing to pay the price. A lasting relationship involves sacrifice, serving, giving, and forgiving. Marriage takes work, commitment, and courage. It takes addressing the twelve problems discussed in this book. Be willing to talk about the problems and their solutions. Remember that the goal of a successful marriage is for husband and wife to become their best friends.

Although twelve problems have been identified in this book as enemies of happy marriages, there are other problems which time and space would not permit us include. These include excessive debt/credit, abuse and misuse of money, interference from in-laws, incompatibility, putting sex on the back burner, domestic violence, drug and alcohol abuse, boredom, unrealistic expectations, and the list continues. I believe that these problems are not as devastating on your marriage as the twelve mentioned in the book. The problems addressed in this book are the top 12 problems. If you overcome them, others will take care of themselves. If you address them or avoid them, you will enjoy your marriage and be happy. As Albert Einstein said, "A clever person solves a problem. A wise person avoids it."

INDEX